CRE🏠TIVE
HOMEOWNER®

design ideas for
Home Decorating

CREATIVE HOMEOWNER®, Upper Saddle River, New Jersey

CRE🏠TIVE
HOMEOWNER®

A Division of Federal Marketing Corp.
Upper Saddle River, NJ

DESIGN IDEAS FOR HOME DECORATING
SENIOR EDITOR: Kathie Robitz
SENIOR DESIGNER: Glee Barre
DESIGNER: Kathryn Wityk
AUTHOR: Heidi Tyline King
EDITORIAL ASSISTANTS: Jennifer Calvert (proofreading),
    Robyn Poplasky (photo research)
INDEXER: Schroeder Indexing Services
ALL COVER PHOTOGRAPHY (except as noted): Mark Samu; courtesy of Ethan
    Allen (*front bottom left*); Picking Flowers/Sweet Life, courtesy of Thibaut
    (*front bottom right*)

CREATIVE HOMEOWNER
PRESIDENT: Brian Toolan
VP/EDITORIAL DIRECTOR: Timothy O. Bakke
PRODUCTION MANAGER: Kimberly H. Vivas
ART DIRECTOR: David Geer
MANAGING EDITOR: Fran J. Donegan

Printed in China

Current Printing (last digit)
10 9 8 7 6 5 4 3 2 1
Design Ideas for Home Decorating, First Edition
Library of Congress Control Number: 2006924719
ISBN-10: 1-58011-313-3
ISBN-13: 978-1-58011-313-7

CREATIVE HOMEOWNER®
A Division of Federal Marketing Corp.
24 Park Way
Upper Saddle River, NJ 07458
www.creativehomeowner.com

Dedication

For all the do-it-yourselfers
who work hard to turn their houses
into comfortable homes.

Contents

Introduction 6

Chapter 1
Design Basics 8
- what is design?
- know your space
- color, pattern, and texture
- know your style

Chapter 2
Furnishings 46
- furniture decisions
- quality
- lighting
- art and accessories

Chapter 3
Windows and Surfaces 78
- window dressing
- walls
- floors

Chapter 4
Gathering Places 112
- living rooms
- family rooms
- fun and games

Chapter 5
Kitchens 136
- traditional
- country
- contemporary
- cabinets
- wall treatments
- flooring
- ceilings
- countertops

Chapter 6
Bath Style 194
- define the look
- vanities
- bathroom furniture
- walls
- window treatments

Chapter 7
Bedrooms 236
- your sanctuary
- a quality sleep
- kids' rooms
- baby rooms

Chapter 8
Workspaces 268
- the dedicated home office
- the kitchen office

Chapter 9
Outdoor Style 284
- dressing up the outdoors
- porches and sunrooms

Resource Guide 298

Glossary 306

Index 308

Photo Credits 318

ABOVE A fireplace is a lovely architectural feature that deserves to be the focal point in a room.

RIGHT Metallic finishes are popular today and can be found in unexpected places.

BELOW Fabrics play an important role in decor. These alternate patterns in red add interest on dining room chairs.

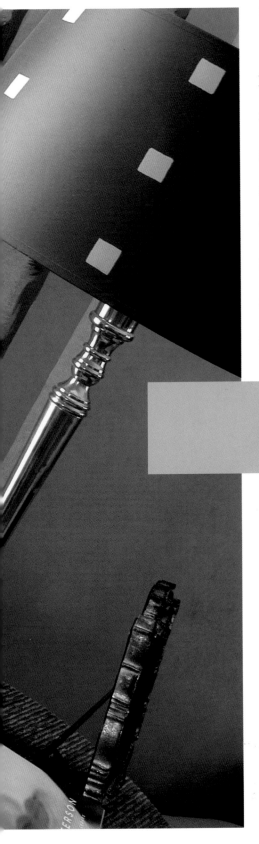

To think of the houses and rooms you have loved is to begin the process of creating your own decorating guidebook. A friend's living room where you gathered for hot cider one chilly Christmas Eve; the guest room at a bed-and-breakfast with linens so soft you wanted to stay under the covers for days; your grandmother's back porch and the table where she dished up homemade ice cream—places such as these live in our memory and ultimately become the yardstick by which we measure all places of comfort and serenity. *Design Ideas for Home Decorating* helps you make the most of your decorating options by pre-

Introduction

senting an array of ideas from a variety of lifestyles that are easy to emulate in your own home. The book begins with the basics—how to work with space. Then you'll learn about furnishings and get the scoop on color. Finally, there are complete chapters devoted to the rooms of your home, each with bright ideas and informative captions that highlight creative options. Above all, *Design Ideas for Home Decorating* encourages you to experiment so that comfort and style blend into a well-loved and personable environment—your home.

Design is much more than making a space look good—it is about celebrating your personality and style. It is about setting a mood and surrounding yourself with the things you love. The easiest way to begin any design project is to figure out what you want to accomplish. Do you want a cheerful room for informal entertaining? Do you need space for work or hobbies? Do you like to host formal dinner parties? Do you want to combine the different interests of your family into a cohesive setting? Whatever your intent, this chapter will share key design rules to get you started.

Design Basics

**I what is design? I know your space I
I color, pattern, and texture I
I know your style I**

Developing an eye for decorating is as simple as knowing your style and favorite color schemes, plus learning how to use the simple basic guidelines of good design.

what is design?

Design is simply a way of creating functional, attractive space. A basic framework for good design involves a few fundamental principles, such as scale and proportion, line, balance, harmony, and rhythm. Color, pattern, and texture are other aspects of design that can add complexity and sophistication to a room. How you interpret these principles is a matter of taste and preference. Indeed, rooms with style should reflect your personality and interests. So the best way to make your foray into decorating is by determining the mood you want to set, from whimsical to French country to 1950s glamour, to name a few. Then turn to the things you love—your garden, a pretty tablecloth, the color of snow-capped mountains—to inspire your vision.

If you feel overwhelmed, start by clearing the room of all the furnishings. This way you can observe the true architectural nature of the space without distractions that can influence your perceptions. For example, without curtains, you can see that two windows may be slightly different sizes or that heat registers are conspicuously located. After a few days, add back the furniture gradually to determine what you like well enough to keep for use in your new design.

OPPOSITE The choice of fabrics and colors in a contemporary living room are peaceful and serene. To keep the look from becoming bland—and to reflect the homeowner's sense of style—a fine art collection is showcased on the walls around the room.

ABOVE LEFT Built-in cabinetry is a luxurious necessity. Because books line most of the shelves, a seating area in front is appropriate for readers in the family.

ABOVE RIGHT A massive fireplace poses a true design challenge of scale and proportion. Overhead lighting highlights the area as a focal point but also lightens the dark tones in the stone. Another trick to help unify the fireplace with the rest of the room is to use light colors found in the stone as an all-over palette.

RIGHT Horizontal stripes look contemporary, in keeping with the rest of the room's decor.

know your space

Before you begin, look around and assess the space you want to decorate. Chances are good there are some things you like about the existing space as well as things you don't like. The windows may overlook a beautiful view, or the room might have a spacious floor plan; but perhaps there are too many doorways or not enough wall space for placing furniture. Or maybe the room is long and narrow with low ceilings that give it a boxed-in feel. Unless structural changes are an option, you will have to figure out how to make some of the negative aspects of the room disappear and find ways to take more advantage of some of the room's best attributes.

Begin by making a list of all the things you like and dislike. Think about how you will use the space, whether you need to consider privacy in your design, whether the light is adequate, and how the traffic moves into and within the room. Compile a notebook with your lists, and add in paint chips and fabric and wallpaper samples. It is also helpful to look through books and magazines to find examples of rooms that may be similar to your own. Tear out the pictures that you especially like, and tuck them into your notebook. Take good measurements of your space, and sketch your plan on paper. Having concrete specifications and a written plan will help you to solidify what works in the existing space and what will need refinement.

OPPOSITE TOP LEFT AND RIGHT
The best way to tackle a large room is by dividing the space into smaller areas—rooms within a room.

OPPOSITE BOTTOM A massive stone fireplace flanked by floor-to-ceiling windows needs little embellishment.

ABOVE Sometimes a large room can be challenging for furniture arranging. Use a rug to anchor a seating area.

RIGHT Choose furniture based on the room's scale. This entertainment center is tall and bulky—the right proportions for a room this size.

the fundamentals that apply

Even if you are not familiar with the fundamental principles of design, you will know when they are used effectively in a room because it looks and feels right.

Scale refers to the size of an object as it relates to the size of everything else in the room. **Proportion** is the relationship of parts or objects to one another based on size—the size of the window is in proportion to the size of the room, for example. Good scale is achieved when all parts are proportionately correct relative to each other and to the whole.

Line defines space. Two-dimensional space consists of flat surfaces, such as walls, floors, and ceilings. Adding depth to a flat surface creates three-dimensional space—the

combination of walls, floor, and ceiling makes a room.

Balance makes the relationship between objects seem natural and comfortable to the eye. All furnishings, large and small, should be distributed evenly throughout a room.

Symmetry refers to the same arrangement of parts, objects, or forms on both sides of an imagined or real center line. Asymmetry is the balance between objects of different sizes as the result of placement.

Harmony is achieved when all elements coordinate with each other. Rhythm refers to repeated patterns. The key to creating good harmony and rhythm is balance; always add at least one contrasting element for interest.

OPPOSITE The rectangular panels in the door are mimicked by the rectangular shape of the picture frames, an effective use of pattern and rhythm.

LEFT Unusually high ceilings and a soaring stone fireplace dominate this large open-plan living room. The asymmetrical hearth is contemporary and less formal looking than a classic fireplace design.

BELOW Cool blue fabric lends a harmonious feel to this room. Note the symmetrical arrangement of furniture around the fireplace. The painting's large scale suits the room's height, too.

bright idea

tall order

Visually raise the height of a room with a low ceiling by incorporating vertical lines into your decorating scheme. Draw the eye upward with vertical striped wallpaper or fabric, tall columns, fluted pilasters, or an arrangement of wall art.

IIIII good design is pleasing to the eye IIIIIIIIIIIIIIIIIIIIIIIII

ABOVE Large rooms can feel cavernous and tip the balance of scale and proportion. Combat the tendency by breaking up the space into several functional areas. In this corner, a daybed provides a place to sleep or lounge.

OPPOSITE TOP LEFT A simple desk becomes a more substantial element in the design scheme when topped with tall lamps and skirted with creamy linen, hiding the file cabinets.

OPPOSITE TOP RIGHT The symmetrical arrangement of objects on the mantel enhance this fireplace's classic style.

OPPOSITE BOTTOM In a room with high ceilings and paneled walls, the low-seated furniture could easily disappear, save for the arrangement of square frames above the sofa. The frames fill the void of space between the visual planes of the ceiling and the furniture.

bright idea

balancing act

When a piece of furniture looks out of place, use accessories to balance the piece within the space. For example, add pillows to either end of a sofa for visual width, a rug to draw the eye downward, or a tall vase or lamp to add height to a low table.

color, pattern, and texture

Color can instantly change the look and feel of a room. It is also a quick way to incorporate personality into your decor. But because of its boldness and striking results, color remains one of the most daunting challenges for some. One way to ease into the world of color is by using a color wheel, which is illustrated on page 20. The color wheel lets you see what colors work well in combination. Another way is to play with different shades or tones of the same color. If you use more than one color, stick with the same intensity. In other words, don't use deep green with a pale yellow.

Along with color, introduce *pattern* to energize your room. Use one pattern throughout for drama and strength, or mix and match for a lively effect. Manufacturers of both wallpaper and fabric make it easy to coordinate patterns and prints by offering groupings of three or four motifs with common elements that tie them together. If you try mixing and matching on your own, choose a recurring theme or color. Avoid using more than one pattern of similar scale. Pair a large motif with a small print, for example.

Finally, *texture* may not have the obvious impact on a room that color and pattern do, but this ingredient can subtly lift a ho-hum design into a sophisticated stratosphere. A mix of textures plays upon the senses and adds another layer of complexity to a scheme. To give a room distinctive character, layer contrasting textures from fabrics, floorcoverings, wall finishes, and window treatments.

OPPOSITE Pink and orange pillows give this otherwise monochromatic room a dash of bold, fun color. Each color is used throughout the room, but this daybed is the only place they are combined, a move that makes the arrangement all the more powerful.

ABOVE Formal floor-to-ceiling curtains in orange and white might easily appear overwhelming. Yet because the pattern is used sparingly, the curtains frame the windows with comfortable, easy elegance without detracting from the overall decorating scheme.

LEFT A tiled stone countertop lends natural warmth and timeless appeal to the kitchen. Its cleft surface provides textural contrast to the sleek, contemporary accessories in stainless steel and punchy orange.

Color Wheel Combinations

What you see as different colors are actually different wavelengths of light. The color wheel is a tool for pairing colors. It presents the spectrum of hues as a circle. The primary colors (yellow, blue, and red) are combined in the remaining hues (orange, green, and purple). Here are common color scheme configurations.

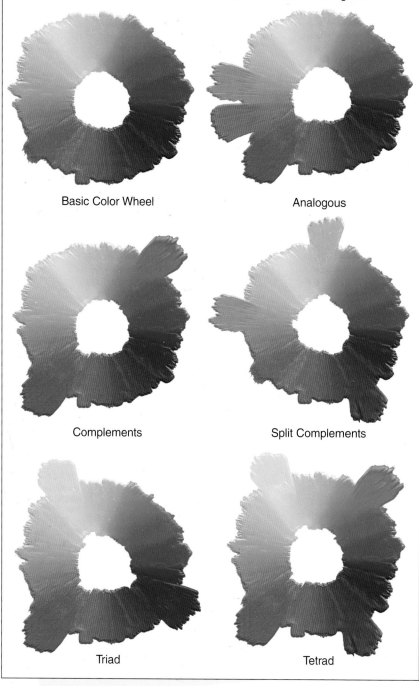

Basic Color Wheel

Analogous

Complements

Split Complements

Triad

Tetrad

OPPOSITE Bright orange tulips (left) and pale violet lilacs (right) illustrate the opposite moods that are evoked by colors on different sides of the color wheel. Warm orange, which is a mixture of red and yellow, is energized and extroverted. The yellow-green color of the apples adds a lively contrast. On the other hand, cool pale violet, which combines red and blue tinted with white, appears rather shy.

how to **w**ork with the **c**olor **w**heel

Every color has inherent evocative characteristics. For example, red is typically very stimulating, so it is a good choice for the dining room, where lively conversation is key to an entertaining dinner party. On the other hand, blue is restful, hence its popularity for use in the bedroom. But your individual response to a particular color is deeply personal. That is why it is important to include the colors you love in your decor. Your wardrobe, the fabric on your existing furniture, and even the color of your current rooms will give you insight into the colors that naturally appeal to you—and what colors you do not like. But it's also important to choose the right color for the room your are decorating.

Also, look at the color wheel to see how colors relate to each other. The color wheel includes all the *primary colors* (red, blue, and yellow); *secondary colors* (green, orange, and violet), which are made by combining two primaries; and *tertiary* colors, which mix a primary with a secondary color. For example,

the tertiary color turquoise is created by mixing the primary color blue with the secondary color green.

A *harmonious* or *analogous* scheme involves neighboring colors that share an underlying hue. Choose one dominant color, then pick accents from adjacent colors. *Contrasting,* or *complementary,* colors, such as blue and orange, lie opposite each other and often work well together. Sometimes you have to play with various shades and tints of complementary colors so they won't overpower a room.

A *double-complementary* color scheme involves an additional set of opposites, such as green-blue and red-orange.

A *monochromatic scheme* can be boring, so introduce several tints or several shades of the color. But avoid too many contrasting values, which can make a color scheme look uneven.

▌▌▌ color can work magic if you know a few tricks ▌▐▐▐▐▐▐▐▐▐▐▐▐▐▐

bright idea

colorize it

If you are decorating a large room, such as a family room with a vaulted ceiling, use warm colors, which appear to advance. This will make the room feel more intimate. Conversely, cool tones and neutrals appear to recede and can be used to make a small room, such as a hallway, seem larger.

light colors advance, dark colors recede

OPPOSITE An ordinary staircase is dramatic and defined by the stark contrast of white walls and stair risers against the walnut stair treads, banister, and black stair runner.

ABOVE A small bedroom benefits from the repetition of pattern and color found on the table skirt, bed canopies, and pillows. White matelassé bedding also contributes to the visual expansion of the room.

RIGHT Terra-cotta-color walls, dark woods, upholstery— even the neutral shades on the window bring warmth to an oversized living room. Touches of complementary color on the pillows, framed art, and window treatments keep the color scheme from becoming too dark and heavy.

play it up with pattern

What fun a room becomes when pattern plays throughout the decor. Like warm colors, large patterns fill a space, usually making a large room seem cozy. They also create a lively and stimulating atmosphere. You can use large patterns in small areas as well, an option that is especially effective when you stick with one pattern and use it throughout the room. Take care not to overpower the room with a pattern that is too bold (out of proportion), however.

Small-scale patterns appear to recede, making small spaces seem larger. They can be used to camouflage odd angles or corners, such as an attic ceiling. Try a subtle, nondirectional pattern for this kind of application. In a large room, the effect of a small pattern is minimal because it is hard to interpret when viewed from a distance. A good rule of thumb is to use large patterns on large-size furnishings, medium prints on medium pieces, and small prints on accent pieces.

LEFT This floral pattern can be used in a large or small room because of its white background. Choose colors found in the motif for accent paint colors and fabrics.

OPPOSITE TOP All-white rooms have a clean, airy feel but can be void of personality. Incorporating several patterns on the upholstery adds style and interest without detracting from the lightness of the room.

OPPOSITE BOTTOM Snappy geometric fabric on a pillow accomplishes a playful twist on formality by adding a sense of whimsy, comfort, and easy elegance.

RIGHT Floor-to-ceiling white curtains fade into the background save for their eye-popping pattern-repeating blue rings. Their placement above the lower portion of an arched-top window adds definition and visually lowers the ceiling.

touch of texture

Looks aren't everything, especially when it comes to texture. This element of design is subtle but essential—it gives your decorating project depth and dimension. The easiest way to incorporate texture into a design is with fabric. Brocades and damasks, moirés and chenilles, tweeds and chintzes—all conjure up different looks and sensations. Fabrics, however, are just the beginning. Tactile interest can emanate from any material or surface that is coarse or smooth, hard or soft, matte or shiny. Remember: coarse and matte surfaces, such as stone, rough-hewn wood, stucco, corduroy, or terra-cotta, absorb light and sound. Glossy and smooth surfaces, such as metal, glass, silk, and enamel, reflect light.

ABOVE LEFT Faux alligator wallcovering adds interest to this foyer wall. On the table, notice the play of complementary textures; the light sheen of pottery, the coarse warmth of wood, the cool smoothness of marble. Combining textures, even when they are in the same color family, adds complexity to the composition of a room.

ABOVE RIGHT This time it's a faux grass-weave wallcovering that makes a subtle but definite statement on its own while allowing the carving and ornament on the white fireplace to stand out with distinction.

OPPOSITE A rustic country living room relies on the textures of natural materials, such as wood, foliage, linen, and rattan, to make it casual and inviting.

LEFT Inspired by art, red is a natural choice for an accent color in this room.

ABOVE Wallpaper with a Chinese red background warms a country dining room. Blue and white pottery adds a contrasting note of color.

BELOW The welcoming pale peach walls of a room are toned down with natural wood tones and white curtains.

OPPOSTE TOP Red stands out against a background of white walls.

OPPOSITE BOTTOM Solid and patterned fabrics can be stylishly mixed.

||| rooms come alive with red and orange ||||||||||||||||||||||||

red and orange

Medical tests have proved that the color red can increase a viewer's heart rate and raise body temperature. No wonder, then, that this power color is a good choice for rooms used for activities. As the dominant color in a room, red is lively, intense, and bold. As an accent color, red adds punch to a decor.

Orange is a mix of red and yellow, and therefore takes on characteristics of both. It is as energetic as red, but more cheerful like yellow. Orange is a good color to use when you need to brighten a space. If used throughout a room, choose a lighter shade to keep the color from appearing too harsh.

blue and purple

Borrowed from nature's palette, blue is one of the best ways to bring the beauty and serenity of nature indoors. To paint a room blue is to create a restful, cool, and fresh environment—that's why you often see blue in bedrooms. Blue also creates an illusion of space and distance, so rooms painted blue actually look and feel larger than they are.

Purple, or violet, combines the intensity of red with the soothing quality of blue. Passionate and regal, the deepest purple creates rooms that are charged with emotion.

emote in blue and princely purple

ABOVE LEFT A soft blue complements an all-white color scheme without detracting from its crisp, clean feel.

ABOVE You can never go wrong with sky blue. Here, it becomes the backdrop for a sea-and-sky-inspired mural.

LEFT An interesting combination of purple and blue dresses a sitting room.

OPPOSITE Cool blue is easy on the eye and restful. Here, pale green accents were inspired by the fabric's print.

green and **y**ellow

When you want to create peaceful surroundings for yourself, take a cue from nature and turn to the color green. Like blue, green is restful and calming, and there are limitless shades to play with to achieve the look you want to convey. Green works well as the dominant color or accent in a room.

At its fullest intensity, yellow is brilliant and lively, the perfect color for a room that is dark, without windows, or in need of an uplifting color scheme. When muted, yellow has a calm, refreshing feel and can be used in virtually any room in your home.

LEFT Green and gold upholstery injects color into a room without upsetting the natural color palette.

RIGHT The furniture and accessories in this room play off the warm, rich ambiance created by golden walls.

BELOW A ceiling painted a lovely sage green looks smart and attractive in an otherwise pale-yellow scheme.

OPPOSITE The glorious olive-green walls and unadorned windows work in concert to bring the outdoors inside.

refresh any room with yellow and green

I I I I I I I **capitalize on the nuance of neutrals and naturals** I I I I I

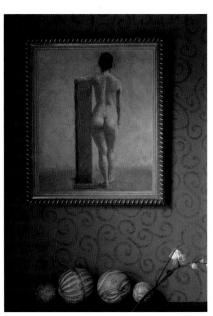

OPPOSITE FAR LEFT An all-white still life of coral, flowers, and pottery creates a sublime arrangement against a creamy off-white wall.

CENTER A neutral color scheme depends on diversifying the texture in a room to provide interest. Here, silk curtains, knobby upholstery fabric, sleek leather, warm wood, and translucent lamp shades work in tandem.

LEFT Inspired by the art, the tone-on-tone gray wallpaper looks elegant.

OPPOSITE BOTTOM LEFT Natural wood warms this neutral color palette.

OPPOSITE BOTTOM RIGHT Beige and white create a serene bedroom retreat.

BELOW There is no more classic color combination than black and white.

neutrals and naturals

Neutral color schemes can be dramatic and sophisticated. Because the color palette is limited, these monochromatic decors are easy to pull together and extremely effective when refinement and taste are the goals for your room. Neutrals and naturals rely on texture, pattern, and contrast for depth and interest. They are also appropriate when you have an attractive piece of furniture or an interesting collection to highlight. The best results are achieved when there is one dominant neutral in the room, on either the furniture and window treatments or the walls. Add a darker neutral for contrast; then fill in with a third or fourth neutral to round out the look. If the room becomes monotonous or bland, give it a shot of color—one color—that is used sparingly as an accent.

bright idea

tone and shade

In color-talk, what's the difference between a tone and a shade? Mix white with any hue to tone it down. The lightest tone of a color is called pastel. If you mix black into a color, you'll create a darker shade of that hue.

LEFT Images splashed across pale pink wallpaper are the impetus for the yellow curtains and pastel blue chair.

BELOW LEFT Pale spring green becomes a neutral when set against off-white countertops and backsplashes in this kitchen.

BELOW RIGHT A light yellow softens the denim blue used throughout this nursery.

OPPOSITE Hybrids of the more intense colors on the color wheel, pastels soften a decorating scheme.

ABOVE Chocolate-color walls make this guest room snug.

ABOVE Vivid blue and crisp white look sublime together.

IIII enhance the drama using colors with intensity and depth II

bright idea

fearless color

Balance deep color with light accessories and furnishings. White-painted or light natural wood tones pair well with intense shades. In general, limit deep colors to areas that receive lots of light or a single accent wall.

ABOVE Red raspberry walls don't overpower the decor thanks to generous light.

OPPOSITE An intense shade of green wraps this sitting room in luxurious color.

What is your style? If you are like most people, it's easier to say what it's not than what it actually is. You may know that you don't like plaid or that yellow is your least-favorite color. While these hint at what your true style is, it is helpful to create a scrapbook or binder that illustrates exactly what types of interiors make you feel most at home. Cut out specific pictures—chairs, beds, rugs, or even accessories—that speak to you. Create one page for color, pasting in samples of paints and fabrics. Once you look at your collection, you will notice common themes that are clues to your personal style.

find your style

Armed with the knowledge of what furnishings, fabrics, colors, and objects you like and what style you want to reflect in your home, go shopping—at home and in stores. Look at the furnishings and accessories you have that are in keeping with your identified style, and discard those that don't. You will then have an idea of what items you might consider purchasing to enhance your style.

While structure gives you a foundation, no style is complete without personal touches. Look at souvenirs you have gathered on trips, favorite rugs or blankets, family photos, and interesting objects that have a sense of personality and use them throughout your decor.

▌▌▌ classic looks never go out of fashion ▌▌▌▌▌▌▌▌▌▌▌▌▌▌▌▌▌▌▌▌▌▌▌

OPPOSITE Unpretentious but eye-catching, a zippy carpet runner lends fun and informality to an otherwise traditional entry hall.

ABOVE A neutral color scheme, skirted table, and understated chandelier suggest an updated take on a classic look.

LEFT The formal French air of this living room takes its cue from the ornate molding in the room. The yellow-green fabrics add a fresh note.

||||| the fresh face of contemporary style |||||||||||||||||||||

ABOVE LEFT Minimal accessories, natural wood finishes, and unadorned glass are all characteristics of modern decoration.

ABOVE Contemporary homes are open and airy, with little embellishment on the furniture or interior trim work.

LEFT Diversity in materials rather than decoration gives continuity, depth, and interest to contemporary rooms.

OPPOSITE The play of line is important in a contemporary home. The bench, low-slung sofa, stairs, and cabinet all have lines that create interesting contrast in the room.

bright idea
declutter

Simplicity is key in clean-lined modern interiors. To update your look, get rid of clutter: stacks of magazines, knickknacks, and anything else that doesn't serve a purpose in a room. After you've paired down, install streamlined built-in cabinetry to keep rooms orderly and your stuff out of sight.

LEFT Plain windows, pretty flowers, potted plants, a distressed bench, and a painted floor give this entry a casual country look.

mix it up

When you pick and choose your favorite design elements from several different styles, the outcome is not always predictable, but it is almost certainly more interesting. That's because rather than being dictated by the rules of a particular style, your personal likes and dislikes become the measure for decorating.

If you like a laidback living room but don't want the "shabby chic" look, build a contemporary setting with sleek lines but add pillows on furniture and the floor to soften the look and invite lounging. An old-fashioned kitchen can have turquoise cabinetry and still maintain its ode to the past. Dare to try something different!

ABOVE A room swathed in toile is French country in the purest sense. Adding wicker suitcases, wrought iron, and wood plays up the informality of a country interior.

OPPOSITE TOP In classic American-country style, this dining room is welcoming, with its large wooden table and ladder-back chairs.

OPPOSITE LEFT The river-rock fireplace and rough-hewn mantel typify cabin style.

OPPOSITE RIGHT A painted desk in this tangerine-color hallway looks charming in a cottage-inspired home.

choose from a variety of country-inspired styles

2

Furniture is an important decorating element. Not only must furniture reflect your personal taste and the style you want to convey, but it has to be comfortable. Cost, of course, is a factor, but paying top dollar doesn't always mean you're buying the best—only quality materials and reliable construction can ensure that. Remember durability when you're choosing furniture. If you have children or expect to use the furniture daily, select pieces that are sturdy and avoid delicate fabrics and finishes. This chapter will help you choose furniture that is right for your space and lifestyle.

Furnishings

I furniture decisions I quality I
I lighting I art and accessories I

Furnishing your home properly will let you express your personal style and allow you to provide the ultimate comfort for your family and guests.

ABOVE Armoires and desks with hutches can seem large and bulky, traits that can overwhelm some spaces. Choosing a desk with open shelving and painting it white avoids this common design problem.

ABOVE A wooden cabinet that holds electronic equipment is proof that storage doesn't have to be ordinary.

RIGHT An oversize sofa with upholstery that complements the wall color provides comfortable seating and blends well with other decorating elements in the room.

furniture decisions

Furniture has three basic functions: providing for seating, sleeping, and storage. The placement of each piece, or the furniture layout, is dependent on the room's shape. Long, narrow spaces work better when divided into distinct areas for different functions. Square rooms offer the option of grouping furniture in the middle of the room.

Layout is determined by a room's function. In a bedroom, the bed takes center stage, with storage and perhaps a sitting area, a media cabinet, or in the case a desk somewhere for a student. The living room may have a variety of functions from watching TV with the family to entertaining friends. Think about how you use your living room to help guide your decision in deciding on a layout.

Indirectly, furniture can be used to efficiently divide space. Within a large room, you could create a cozy sitting area in front of a fireplace and place an entertainment center in another area. Or if you need to define separate living and dining areas within one space, a sofa with a low back can act as a divider, as can an étagère, a decorative screen, or a long table. Modular seating pieces are particularly practical if your need your layout to be flexible.

Always carefully consider the size of any furniture that you are considering for purchase. Furniture pieces that are the right scale and in proportion with one another and the space will not only look great together but add to the comfort and function of a room.

ABOVE These handsome club chairs were upholstered in soft, supple, and durable leather. Buy the best quality furniture possible for longevity. In the case of leather, choose top grain. Upholstery fabric should be treated with a stain guard.

LEFT Casters that double as feet give this piece of furniture multiple uses. Place it by a bed as a nightstand, or roll it across the room for use next to a desk as additional work space or storage. Because of their modernity, casters also give the room an up-to-date look.

OPPOSITE LEFT Another example of casegoods, a chest in a bathroom adds warmth and a place for linens.

OPPOSITE RIGHT A charming cupboard is a handsome addition to this room, providing much-needed storage. Glass doors on top display collections, and sliding doors on the bottom hide useful but less-attractive items.

furniture types and terms

The furniture industry uses a variety of terms to label and categorize furniture. Here are some common ones:

Modular An unlimited number of pieces that can be used in a number of different configurations. Modular furniture is almost always upholstered. Sectional sofas are popular modular furniture.

Casegood Casegood refers to any piece of furniture that is used for storage, such as a chest of drawers. Tables are also part of this category, as well as hutches and desks. The name is derived from the box-like shape of most casegoods.

Seating Seating denotes both upholstered and non-upholstered pieces. Chairs and sofas are common pieces in this category.

Movable Movable furniture is exactly that—furniture that can be moved with ease. Look for pieces with rollers and casters that are either fixed or can flip up when not in use.

Built-ins Today's built-ins have advanced far beyond traditional cabinetry. Wall-to-wall shelving, cabinetry with furniture-style feet to resemble buffets and armoires, banquettes, and even fold-away beds are some of the creative options for built-ins.

COM Custom-ordered furniture lets you personalize furniture to your specifications. Options for finishes and fabrics are common, but some manufacturers go so far as to let you pick the feet, trim, shape, and wood for your furniture. This type of furniture is not available on the sales floor and requires a wait before receiving, usually 6 to 12 weeks.

RTA Ready-to-assemble furniture comes in pieces that you put together at home. Because you provide the labor, this type of furniture is usually less expensive. Most RTA furniture is designed to fit into your automobile, which eliminates shipping and transportation costs.

cushion **s**hapes

Upholstered furniture receives much harder wear than almost any other piece of furniture in your home. That's why it is important to choose upholstered pieces that can withstand repeated movement and weight, as well as retain their appearance over time. Frames and springs are the foundation for cushions. A good frame is padded with cotton or polyester batting so that the upholstery fabric never touches the wood. Quality seat cushions and loose back cushions consist of a combination of down and other feathers wrapped around a polyurethane foam core—or loose down or feathers for back cushions.

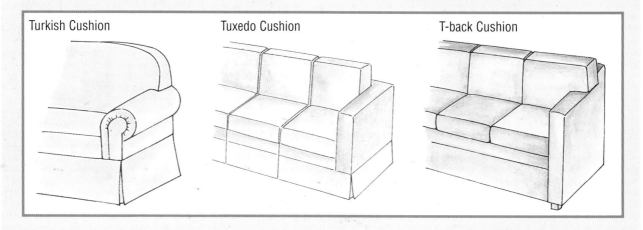

Turkish Cushion   Tuxedo Cushion   T-back Cushion

OPPOSITE Test the quality of a loose cushion to lifting it. If it feels light, it may be made of poor materials. A 2 x 2-foot cushion should not weigh less than 2 lbs.

LEFT Stylized cushions will have more structure, which is created by wrapping a foam base with batting. The cushion might also have some down or loose batting for an oversized effect.

BELOW Upholstered sofas and chairs should provide a sturdy framework for the cushions on top.

quality

When shopping for furniture, don't be shy. Check inside, and look underneath to ensure you are purchasing a well-built piece. Wavy springs and spiral coils are the most common types of suspension for upholstered furniture. Without them, a piece of furniture would sag and lose its shape. In high-quality coil systems, the coils are anchored to the frame eight ways and spaced close together. Flat-double sagless springs should be connected with spiral springs for greater stability.

For fillings, horsehair, straw, down, and cotton flock have been traditional, but polyurethane foam is the most-common filling in today's upholstered furniture. Strong and resilient, it is usually wrapped with another material, such as down or polyester batting, to give it more shape. Foam inserts should have a high density; low-quality foam will not hold its shape and disintegrates quickly.

A piece of furniture's covering has the biggest influence on its price. A tightly woven fabric treated with a stain-resistant coating will last the longest, but you can also opt for fabrics that are easily cleaned with upholstery shampoo or slipcovers that can be removed and laundered. Check construction to ensure that seams are tightly stitched and have an overlock finish that won't fray.

To evaluate the quality of wood furniture, look for strong construction at the joints. They are usually glued together or fastened with screws. Staples should not be used to join any piece of furniture that bears weight.

LEFT Wood furniture should have sturdy, secure joints. Woven seats, like the rush seats on these stools, should have no frayed ends or breaks in the fiber.

OPPOSITE TOP LEFT When metal accents are used on furniture, the metal should be securely fastened to the piece. All edges that meet should be even.

OPPOSITE TOP RIGHT Metal furniture should have even joints and hidden screws to hold the frame together. Joints can also be soldered together for additional strength.

OPPOSITE BOTTOM For upholstered furniture, the seat should be harder than the back of the chair and should resume its shape quickly after you stand up. Press your hand across the chair to make sure all springs are even.

OPPOSITE A formal loveseat is dressed down when covered with a cheery floral print. Because the fabric matches the wallpaper, the loveseat blends into the background of the room, visually enlarging a small corner.

LEFT Pretty dining room chairs with comfortable padding can be moved to other rooms as needed for additional seating. Paint the chairs in complementary colors for interest, and upholster cushions in colorful versions of the same fabric for continuity.

seating

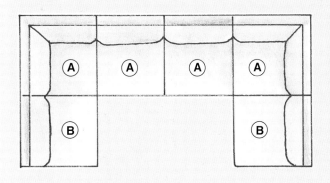

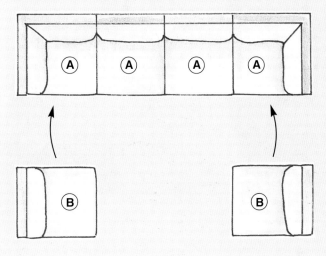

Configuring a successful seating layout can be a challenge. Place large pieces of furniture first so you can determine what other furnishings you might need and how to use the pieces you have. Consider traffic patterns and whether you want an intimate conversation area or need your furniture to fill up an entire room.

U-shaped arrangements provide seating for the greatest number of people. This configuration is cozy and casual and has a "room-within-a-room" effect.

Dividing a sectional creates a traffic pattern and two conversation areas as opposed to one. This is a good arrangement if you have a large room.

An **L-shaped** arrangement works well when you need to make separate activity spaces in an open floor plan. L-shaped seating arrangements also work well when an open flow for traffic is needed from one room to the next.

arrangements for **s**leeping

Furniture for sleeping ranges from futon frames to platform beds and bedsteads with head- and foot-boards. Some bedsteads also include bedside stands, lamps, and built-in storage compartments. Convertible sofa beds offer extra sleeping accommodations for small spaces. Other options are the loft bed, which is on a raised platform and frees the space beneath for other uses; bunk beds; and trundle beds, which slide under another bed when not in use.

Above all, you should choose a bed by its comfort. Test out its quality by lying down—you should not feel any springs, coils, or unevenness in the mattress. Next to consider is size and use. In small rooms, daybeds and bunkbeds provide sleeping without taking up the entire floor space. Canopy beds, poster beds, and beds with bulky head- and foot-boards look proportional when used in large bedrooms. Some rooms need a bed to double as seating. Daybeds and oversized chaise lounges can be used in these rooms.

don't skimp—buy a quality mattress

ABOVE A fun, functional option for children's rooms, bunk beds leave plenty of floor space for playing.

RIGHT A generously-sized bedroom can accommodate a king-size bed and its padded headboard with style and balance.

OPPOSITE By day, a spare room is a quaint sitting area with a fancy daybed for seating. By night, the bed becomes comfortable sleeping quarters for a guest.

LEFT A mirrored buffet elevates the wow factor in a dining room, but indirectly, the middle section provides storage for linens and silver.

bright idea
create storage

Along with furniture, many accessories such as baskets, bins, hatboxes, and trays provide stylish options for storage. Also look for storage potential in a room— baskets under a bed, a shelf mounted above a door, and containers that fit along the tops of cabinetry have the capacity for storage.

storage sense

No one has enough of it—that's why it is important to consider what types of things you need to store before purchasing casegoods. Bookcases or any other type of open shelves are great, but not for clothing, for example. Cabinets with hinged or sliding doors are excellent for housing audio or video equipment. China cabinets and breakfronts provide proper storage and display for place-settings and glassware. Modular pieces can be used as storage walls or room dividers. Storage furniture for the bedroom—dressers, vanities, and chests—are categorized by the size of their contents. Look for ones with several drawer sizes—compact for things like socks, and deep for bulky items, such as sweaters. Many storage pieces can serve multiple purposes. For example, an armoire is typically purchased for the bedroom but can be a helpful addition to a kitchen or bathroom. Built-ins are an alternative to furniture and can hold a variety of items, from books to clothing to entertainment equipment.

OPPOSITE A built-in vanity in a child's room eliminates clutter and streamlines the look of the room. Paint built-ins the same color as the walls so they blend in, or choose a contrasting color to highlight the built-in as a separate design component.

RIGHT When you need more storage in a small room, think vertical. A tall, narrow piece, such as this lingerie chest, takes up little floor space but can hold a lot of items.

reusing old furniture

A coat of paint and new fabric can transform old furniture into stylish conversation pieces. An added bonus is that old furniture is often made of solid wood, which costs a premium in today's furniture market.

OPPOSITE A tufted ottoman has multiple uses, especially if the top is firmly upholstered. Use it for additional seating when it's needed or let your ottoman double as a table.

ABOVE Some styles, like these French-country bergere chairs, are never out of vogue. Simply update the look by re-covering them in buttery leather. Choose a traditional print for a formal room, or a whimsical pattern for fun.

RIGHT Rather than skirt this sofa in the same fabric as the sides and cushions, long, heavy fringe was added to create interest with color and texture.

calculating **y**ardage

Look beyond tattered upholstery to the bones of a piece of furniture. If you see what you like, reupholstering the item can be less or more expensive than purchasing a new piece, depending on the fabric and finishing details. The best way to determine how much fabric you will need for an upholstery project is to measure each section of the piece and combine the total. Add extra yardage for patterns and repeats, and, if desired, purchase extra fabric for accessories such as tablecloths and pillows. The following list is a basic guide to help you figure out— roughly—how much fabric you'll need for your project. This estimate is based on 52-in.-wide fabric.

Wing chair: No skirt, approximately 8 yds.
Club chair: Approximately 7 yds.
Dining chair cushion and back: Approximately 1 ½ yds.
Lawson sofa*: Approximately 14 yds.
Chippendale sofa*: Approximately 12 yds.
Tuxedo sofa*: Approximately 13 yds.
T-cushion contemporary sofa**: Approximately 14 yds.
Queen Anne chair with wooden arms: No skirt, 3 yds.
Sectional sofa: 1 armless unit, 4 yds.; 1 side arm, 6 yds.

** A standard 6-ft. sofa

ABOVE Canister lighting is a discreet way to add both task and indirect lighting to a room. Table lamps may provide accent or task lighting.

lighting

Lighting seems like an obvious element in the design of any space, but unfortunately, it's often an afterthought. Good lighting enhances a room's function and mood, so it deserves your thoughtful consideration.

To formulate a successful lighting plan for your home, make sure that each room has adequate amounts of both indirect light—natural and overhead lighting—and direct light, which is for illuminating work areas or drawing attention to a noteworthy object, such as a painting or objects in a cabinet.

The amount and quality of natural light a room receives depends on the size of its windows and its orientation with regard to the sun. Blocking excessive natural light is easy to do with window treatments, but adding natural light can be a challenge. As a supplement, overhead and direct lighting augments natural light; after dark, it compensates for daylight completely.

Ambient (general) light should surround a room without appearing to come from any one specific direction. Overhead fixtures and sconces are good sources. Task light is primarily functional, illuminating a countertop or a vanity mirror, for example. Accent lighting is dramatic. It focuses the eye on a particular spot or object and offsets the less-exciting indirect light.

ABOVE LEFT A beautiful chandelier is an attractive design feature in a dining room. Use a minimum of 150 watts and a maximum of 200 to 300 watts to light a table. To control the light level and set the mood, install a dimmer switch.

ABOVE An art collection hanging in a hallway is illuminated by simple low-votage spotlights.

LEFT A table lamp with an opaque shade that diffuses the light so that it doesn't glare can invite cozy relaxation, socializing, or quiet reading. This particular lamp features an elaborately carved and painted base and a lavish fringed shade—details that tie in with the other design features in the room.

how to select the right lampshade

Furniture may be the focus of a room, but a well-dressed lamp is a stylish, dramatic accent. The difficult challenge, however, is not choosing a pretty shade but selecting one that is right for the lamp and serves your lighting needs at the same time. The more decorative the base of the lamp, the plainer a shade should be. If the base is painted ceramic or carved, go for a classic, tailored shade with clean lines. If the base is a simple candlestick, make a statement with a shade that is frilly or floral. Opaque shades focus the light in one direction, usually down, while translucent shades diffuse light that beams in every direction. Be careful about color: dark-color shades direct light to seating level, while light-color ones create a soft ambient glow.

TOP Stripes of orange ribbon add a punch of color to an otherwise simple, tailored lampshade.

LEFT Chic and modern, aluminum pendant lamps add much-needed contrast to a dining room's dark wood table and chairs.

ABOVE Small lights installed under the wall-mounted cabinets brighten the dark countertop without creating an unattractive glare.

ABOVE An elegant crystal chandelier is the perfect touch over the tub in this bathing alcove.

LEFT An Italian-glass shade used with a chrome sconce adds a dash of color to the neutral tile in this bathroom.

RIGHT These glass pendant lamps exude a timeless, retro look. Pendants are perfect in a kitchen, used over a table or an island.

ABOVE In a circular garden room completely surrounded by windows, lighting hidden behind molding and used to illuminate a sky mural on the ceiling adds to the illusion of being outdoors.

creative lighting

Lighting options are limitless, especially when you are looking for a creative way to illuminate a room. One of the most stunning effects is an illuminated ceiling cove, valance, or soffit, which will highlight a room's architectural features. Fixtures designed for this purpose create dramatic reflective light. Coves distribute light upward. Soffits distribute light downward. Valances distribute light both up and down. A shield, usually made of a piece of wood or plaster molding, hides the light source. Baffles, louvers, or diffusers direct light and reduce glare. You might also consider installing lighting along the top or bottom of cabinetry or inside the cove of a raised ceiling. Integrate a lighted valance with a vaulted ceiling or a curtain sweep; vertically light a wall niche; and highlight molding.

Another effective use of light is to use fixtures in unconventional ways. Portrait lights, normally used to highlight objects and artwork, look smart and streamlined when they are installed above bathroom mirrors. Pendant lights hanging at eye level beside a chair can replace traditional table lamps in dramatic fashion. And under-cabinetry lighting, usually reserved for kitchens, can be installed within a hutch in dining rooms or inside an armoire that may be doubling as a fold-away desk.

RIGHT Double sconces strategically placed beside a foyer mirror add a distinct style to a home's entryway.

ntroducing character into your home may be harder to achieve but more pleasing than simply creating an attractive space. While crown molding, handsome furniture, and attractive window treatments may contribute to your home's good looks, it is the details—your favorite art and accessories—that will enliven your rooms with personality. But are you confident about choosing and arranging these objects so that they don't look like clutter? On the other hand, a home that is completely spare will look and feel unfinished. To find balance, begin by clearing the room you are decorating of everything but the furniture. Gather the objects that you think you'd like to display. Spread them out so you can see them together; then group like items, such as picture frames or pottery. Use these groupings to create vignettes around the

art and accessories

room—that is, arrangements of like objects placed in close proximity to each other. This design strategy is the first step in formulating a cohesive arrangement.

Another way to make your collections visually pleasing is to play with color, line, and shape. Vary the height of objects so your eye moves around the collection. For example, a tall, curvy vase placed on the side of a hanging mirror ties the wall display to the one on the table. For balance, add similar objects that may vary in size or shape. A composition with a few objects has a clean, architectural look, while a larger grouping of color- or theme-related items has a museum quality about it.

LEFT Accessories skillfully arranged on an antique farm table were chosen to reflect the colors in the wallpaper. The painting's position, low on the wall, makes it part of the tabletop vignette.

ABOVE All of the art and accessories in this room are monochromatic, in keeping with the overall color scheme. But the result is dramatic, particularly because the designer has used scale to make a big statement, hanging large framed prints above the fireplace.

RIGHT A candlestick lamp visually anchors an oversized wall clock to the buffet. Color continuity also plays an cohesive role in this design arrangement.

how to select art

Choose art that appeals to you, not because it matches the room. Look for an affordable orginal work by an up-and-coming artist rather than a copy of a Rembrandt. If the piece is large, keep accessories to a minimum for impact. If you have several small- or medium-size artworks or drawings, place them together for an impressive presentation. If you have a colorful painting, pull touches of the same colors found in the artwork into the accessories in the room, such as flowers, pottery, pillows, throws, and rugs.

If you are displaying drawings or photography, make sure the frame is large enough to accommodate a mat. In general, the frame should be 1 to 3 inches larger than the picture, although a larger mat inside a simple frame is often sleek and dramatic. Frames should coordinate with the style of the decor, or they can introduce a new design element, especially if you plan to group similar items together.

OPPOSITE A vivid painting commands attention with its prominent placement and repetition of theme—a contemporary motif.

ABOVE A grouping of fine art is at home in this antique-filled room. The large 18th-century portrait with a gilded frame dominates the space and sets the formal tone.

LEFT The walls of a stairway and upstairs landing is a gallery of early 20th-centuring advertising posters here. A skylight in the stairwell and recessed eyeball spot-lights illuminate these graphic designs.

LEFT One mirror visually enlarges a space; six compose an artful display. These individual mirrors are exactly the same, but each one casts its own reflection, creating interest within this arrangement.

BELOW An antique mirror with a beveled-glass frame and ornamentation adds glamour to this living room.

add mirrors for light and depth

ABOVE In this dressing room, mirrors in gilded frames have been mounted on the door panels, breaking up the massive appearance of floor-to-ceiling built-in cabinets.

bright idea

careful reflection

A mirror may be decorative and practical. Use a mirror to visually expand a small space, such as a bathroom or entry. Because a mirror is reflective, it can create an illusion of light, but it can also reflect an unsightly view, so be careful where you place it.

ABOVE Architectural molding that has been painted white matches the mantel and other trimwork in this room.

RIGHT A mirror in a painted metal frame provides textural contrast when set against simple white full-length curtains.

the **a**rt of **ar**rangement

It is easy to create an attractive wall display of paintings, photographs, and drawings. Working on a flat surface, lay out each piece, switching them around to form your arrangement. For the best result, work within a geometric frame, as shown, to keep the grouping from looking too rigid or plain. Strike a balance by placing large pieces opposite groups of smaller objects. If you have art with different-size mats, unify the look by placing them in rows.

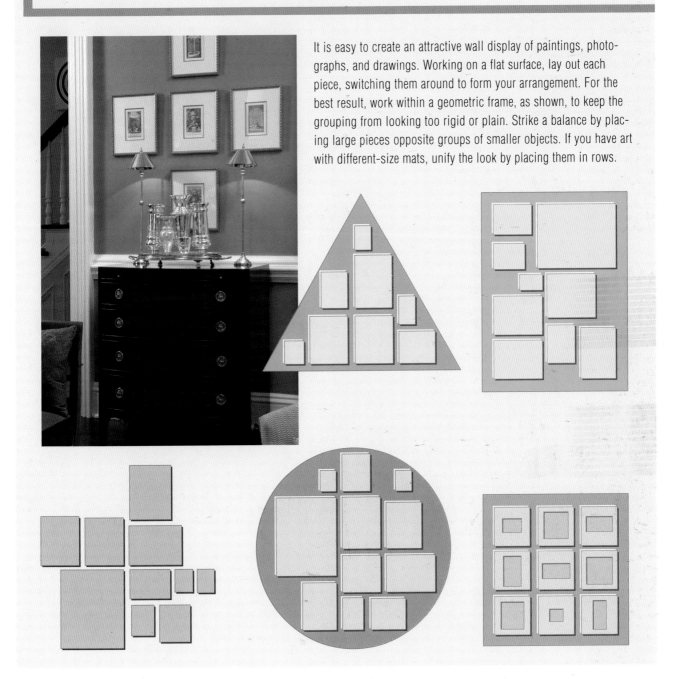

OPPOSITE TOP LEFT Consider textiles when you're looking for art. Here, a gorgeous tapestry, hanging gracefully above a buffet, provides a complex mix of color and pattern.

OPPOSITE TOP RIGHT A small painting on the wall above this mantel display is the focal point of the arrangement. It could be exchanged for a larger painting or framed print that is placed on the mantel and propped against the wall.

OPPOSITE BOTTOM LEFT Rather than compete with the strong, architectural gird created by built-in cubbies, the objects within have curvy shapes for added interest.

OPPOSITE BOTTOM RIGHT Hanging framed prints low on the wall is an effective way to make the bust on the pedestal part of the overall arrangement rather than a separate piece that could distract the eye.

3

When the window, wall, and floor treatments are attractive and functional, decorating the rest of a room becomes less a matter of camouflaging flaws and more about making it look and feel good. Fortunately, wall and window treatments can be easily and usually inexpensively changed as taste dictates or styles change. Indeed, painting a wall and hanging new curtains can deliver a lot of stylish bang for the buck. Flooring, which is typically a permanent feature, can be expensive, however, unless it's a small carpet or area rug that you are replacing. Here are some ideas to get you started.

Windows and Surfaces

▌ window dressing ▌ walls ▌
▌ floors ▌

Walls, windows, and floors create a blank canvas on which to build your decorating scheme. Base your selections on style, care, durability, and function.

window dressing

Frilly, simple, formal, casual, utilitarian, opaque, sheer—avoid being overwhelmed by the variety of window-treatment styles that are available and focus, first, on their purpose and your needs. In addition to its decorative value, the right window treatment attends to practical needs—providing privacy, insulation, ventilation, or light control, to name a few. It may camouflage a less-than-perfect view or visually correct an architectural flaw, such as an opening that is too small or awkward in its location. After you determine what you need from a window treatment, then you can consider the look that best complements your decor. A traditional swag and jabot, with its draped valance and folded panels, adds curve to the boxy outline of a window. A Roman shade is more tailored, fitting over the window completely or inside the frame. Valances used alone can add a simple accent over a window. And blinds and shutters, with their unavoidable play of line, lend a modern flair.

In addition to type, the color and material of a window treatment can make an impact on the decor. Long curtain panels fabricated from fabric that is the same color as the walls will be understated, allowing ornate molding or the view to become the focal point. Bold colors and patterns can make the window the center of attention. An easy way to coordinate upholstered furniture with the window treatment is to use the same or a color- or pattern-related fabric for both.

A well-dressed window can also add texture to an interior: lace softens and soothes; natural materials, such as straw or wood, add earthiness and warmth to a setting. Fabrics like damask, brocade, and taffeta suggest classic elegance, while cotton or linen appear much less formal.

BELOW LEFT The flouncy fullness of a fringed swag and jabot emphasize the period room's romantic feel.

BELOW RIGHT The streamlined structure of matchstick-style Roman shades is in keeping with the clean lines of a modern bath.

OPPOSITE Long silk panels that puddle slightly at the hem look simply elegant in this bedroom.

measuring windows

Correct Measurements will help you determine whether ready-made options will work for you. Without them, you cannot accurately price the elements you need. Use a metal measuring tape for accuracy, and record the measurements on paper.

Inside Mount for Shades, Blinds, and Tension Rods

Inside the window frame, measure the width across the top, center, and bottom. Use the narrowest measurement, and round down to the nearest ⅛ inch. Measure the height of the window from the top of the opening to the sill.

Outside Mount for Shades, Blinds, Cornices, or Curtain or Drapery Rods or Poles

Figure out the amount of space on each side of the window and above and below the window that you want to cover with your treatment. Then decide on bracket placement—on the window frame or the wall.

▌ **Professionals recommend** that outside-mounted shades or blinds extend 2 inches beyond the window sash on each side.

▌ **To determine the appropriate rod length,** measure from bracket to bracket. For a decorative pole with finials, add 5 to 8 inches on each side; the actual amount depends on the finial style. Be sure that you have enough room on either side of the window before you buy the pole and finials.

▌ **For a fuller curtain look,** the width of the panels you use should be at least twice the measurement from bracket to bracket. Some opulent looks call for fabric measuring three times the bracket-to-bracket measurement.

▌ **To determine the appropriate length** of curtain and drapery panels, measure from the bracket placement down to the top of the sill, to below the sill, or to the floor, depending on the length you desire. If the panel heading extends above the rod or pole, add that measurement to the length as well.

RIGHT A draped swag and cascading jabot are tailored to fit in front of a nook of windows but behind an arch that frames the space—and hides the hardware.
▌
OPPOSITE TOP Wooden blinds are a popular choice because of their functionality, easy maintenance, and modern—but warm—appeal.
▌
OPPOSITE BOTTOM Curtains that match the wallpaper fade into the background, making a small neutral living room appear larger than it actually is.

ABOVE Sheer panels hang from a rod above the doors for easy clearance. The half-round is decorative and left unadorned.

which fabric type is right?

The fabric information in the table below will familiarize you with the traditional uses of a variety of materials. The care instructions included in the table are good guidelines, but follow the cleaning instructions given by the manufacturer for any fabric you choose. In addition, always test a sample before cleaning the curtain.

Fabric	Use	Care
Brocade: Weighty fabric in silk, wool, cotton, or a combination featuring a raised (jacquard) design	Draperies and top treatments	Cotton: Machine wash cold / tumble dry low / expect shrinkage Silk: Dry-clean only Wool: Dry-clean only
Cambric: Plain, tightly woven cotton or linen having a sheen on one side	Curtains	Linen: Dry cleaning preferred Hand wash / line dry / may shrink Cotton: Machine wash cold / tumble dry low / expect shrinkage / may lose sheen
Canvas: Coarse, woven cotton; can be heavyweight or lightweight	Curtains, draperies, and shades	Machine wash cold / tumble dry low / expect shrinkage
Chintz: Cotton, all-over print fabric, often floral; coated with a resin that gives it a sheen	Curtains, draperies, and top treatments	Dry-clean only to maintain sheen
Damask: A material made with cotton, silk, wool, or a combination of these fibers with a satin raised (jacquard) design	Draperies and top treatments	See Brocade
Gingham: Plain-woven cotton fabric with block or checked prints	Curtains, draperies, and trimmings	Machine wash cold / tumble dry low / expect shrinkage
Lace: Cotton or a cotton-and-polyester material featuring open-worked designs	Curtains, top treatments, and shades	Some dry-clean only Machine wash cold / gentle cycle / line dry / may shrink
Linen: Strong fabric made from flax; creases easily	Curtains, draperies, and shades	Dry cleaning preferred Hand wash / line dry / expect shrinkage
Moiré: Acetate or silk fabric having a wavy, watermark pattern	Draperies	Dry-clean only
Muslin: A coarse, plain-woven cotton in white or cream; often sheer	Curtains	Machine wash cold / tumble dry low / expect shrinkage
Organdy: Light cotton washed in acid for a crisp finish	Curtains, top treatments, and trimmings	Dry-clean only
Satin: A cotton, linen, or silk fabric with a glossy surface and dull back, sometimes with a moiré finish	Draperies and top treatments	Dry-clean only
Silk: A soft, shiny fabric made from the fine fibers produced by silkworms	Draperies and top treatments	Dry cleaning preferred Hand wash / line dry / expect shrinkage
Taffeta: Acetate or silk fabric that appears shiny and maintains shape	Draperies, top treatments, and trimmings	Dry-clean only
Toile de Jouy: Cotton or linen printed with pastoral scenes	Curtains, draperies, and top treatments	Dry-clean only
Velvet: Cotton, silk, polyester, or viscose rayon fabric with a smooth, iridescent-looking pile	Draperies	Dry-clean only

IIIII for fullness, curtains should be at least twice the width

of the window ▌▌▌▌▌▌▌▌▌▌▌▌▌▌▌▌▌▌▌▌▌▌▌▌▌▌▌▌▌▌▌▌▌▌▌▌▌▌

bright idea
hide in plain sight

You can "equalize" windows that are different sizes by installing the curtain rods at the same height on the wall. This photo illustrates how this trick fools the eye: it's hard to tell, but the window on the right is slightly taller than the one on the left.

curtain panel length

Measure twice is the smartest policy when you are determining the best length for curtain panels, whether you plan to make them or purchase them ready-made. For any type of soft window treatment, measure lengthwise from the intended rod position, whether it will be on the top of the window frame or above the frame on the wall. Full-length panels should slightly puddle on or brush the floor. Apron-length curtains should fall 1 to 4 inches below the windowsill, while sill-length curtains should touch the top of the windowsill.

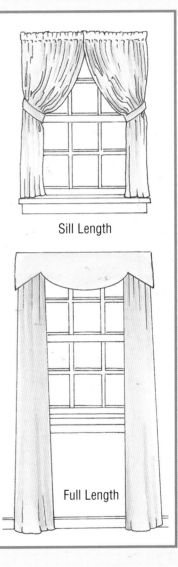

Sill Length

Apron Length

Full Length

OPPOSITE These curtain panels add a much-needed pattern to the room. Curtain rings allow the homeowner to open and close them easily.

ABOVE The right curtain hardware is important. This articulated rod permits someone to open the room to the full view of the window and beyond.

RIGHT An asymmetrical look is a solution when there is limited room on one side of a window to accommodate a curtain with fullness. This pulled-back panel is fixed on the rod, with a semi-sheer treatment underneath for privacy.

OPPOSITE TOP LEFT The no-fuss construction of a Roman shade is ideal for showcasing fabrics with ornate motifs.

OPPOSITE TOP RIGHT A layered look allows for this combination of adjustable room-darkening shades with long curtain panels.

OPPOSITE BOTTOM LEFT Cellular shades filter light without completely darkening a room.

OPPOSITE BOTTOM RIGHT A roller shade with a spring mechanism is ideal for a child's room because it has no cords to pose a safety hazard.

LEFT With its ruffles and gathers, a balloon shade adds a touch of romance paired with full curtain panels.

shades

Shades are a smart, sophisticated way to dress a window. They can be practical, too, because they help to control light and address privacy needs. Most shades fit inside the window frame, which gives them a tailored look. Others are mounted on top of the window frame.

▌ **Cinched shades** have cords to cinch, or pull the fabric upward. These include balloon shades, with billowing festoons; Roman shades that pull up into soft folds; and fan shades that fan out at the ends when the cords are cinched.

▌ **Cellular shades** have a unique honeycomb design that acts as an insulator, trapping air in the middle of the shade that, depending on the season, keeps warm air in or out. Made from a lightweight translucent fabric, these shades filter light even when pulled down.

▌ **Roller shades** consist of a piece of fabric or vinyl attached to a roller that is pulled up with a spring mechanism.

▌ **Shades can be finished** with decorative edgings like fringe, ribbon, and cord to enhance your decor.

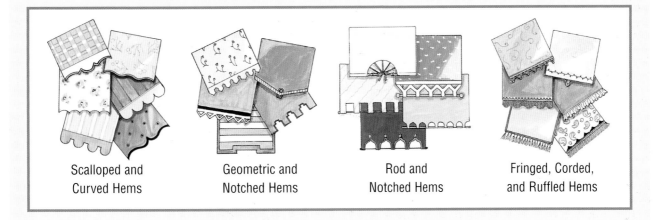

| Scalloped and Curved Hems | Geometric and Notched Hems | Rod and Notched Hems | Fringed, Corded, and Ruffled Hems |

blinds and shutters

When other window treatments fail to produce the desired look or you need a more versatile way to control light, turn to shutters or blinds, another attractive way to dress a window. Blinds, which may be made from metal, wood, or vinyl, can close to block the sun when necessary and provide the utmost privacy when closed. Once considered an expensive choice, the standard-size versions—in particular, vinyl blinds—are reasonably priced and provide a variety of options. Often, contrasting tapes can be added for interest. Use blinds alone for a crisp, modern look, or couple them with other curtains or a valance for a fully dressed window. Shutters are more expensive—usually—than blinds because they are typically custom-fitted to the inside of the window frame. However, there are affordable standard-size shutters on the market, too. Shutters are made of wood or vinyl and have slats that open and close to control light and privacy. Plantation shutters have wide louvers mounted on a fixed frame. Japanese-inspired shoji screens feature a wood lattice design on top of translucent paper. Mounted inside the window frame, they filter light and provide privacy when closed.

Shoji Screens

OPPOSITE TOP LEFT Wood blinds add texture and warmth to a room.

OPPOSITE TOP RIGHT Shutters installed on the lower half of a window provide privacy without blocking natural light.

OPPOSITE BOTTOM LEFT Special shades and blinds can be custom-made to fit roof windows and skylights.

OPPOSITE BOTTOM RIGHT Stacking shutters inside this bay offers even more versatility for light and air control.

LEFT Custom blinds are expensive but can be made to order for hard-to-fit windows, such as an arch or picture window.

ABOVE A pelmet (a valance stretched over a padded wood form) frames the view in this child's room.

OPPOSITE This scalloped valance softens the hard lines of the wooden blinds.

distinctive **v**alances

Valances that are both unique and tasteful can be made from unconventional fabrics, such as scarves. If it's a fabric that you prefer not to cut, drape it around a pole or rod. You can also fold and staple fabric to a mounting board that can be installed above the window. (See the pelmet, above.) Or if it's possible, sew a rod-pocket heading on the fabric. Here are several other suggestions for creating a special valance:

▌ **Hang graduated lengths** of heavy, wide grosgrain ribbons side by side from a rod so that the bottom edges of the ribbons create a shapely form.

▌ **Fold and drape** a fringed shawl, points down, over a rod.

▌ **Tie strings** of beads or seashells onto the ends of a rod, and drape them across the window.

▌ **Use entire or partial pieces** of lace or antique linens that have embroidery, monograms, decorative cutwork, or handmade trimmings to create a valance. Some popular choices include a lace tablecloth or a remnant. You might also consider pillowcases, kitchen towels, or hand towels for narrow windows or the upper portion of an embroidered or eyelet-trimmed flat bed sheet for wide windows. Several linen or cotton napkins or doilies, overlapping each other on a rod, with their corners pointing down, also make charming valances.

hardware

Hardware—rods, poles, rings, sconces, and hold backs—is an important, practical, and often decorative element to be considered when you are selecting most window treatments. Some rods are hidden behind the multiple folds of curtains or slipped through a simple casement running along the top. Others are worthy of showing off, either because of their ornate detailing or contrasting color and texture. Which version is right for your room depends on your taste. If you splurge on fancy rods, highlight them with complementary window treatments. Or in the case of a simple curtain panel, let the style or finish of the hardware create all the drama. Some outstanding decorative hardware on today's market includes designs in various types of metal, glass, enamel, and wood in shiny, matte, or antiqued finishes.

The same is true for hold backs, pins, clips, and rings. Consider these accessories as window jewelry, using them to accentuate your window dressings with a dash of color or shine. One rule of thumb to keep in mind: choose the same finish for hold backs, rods, rings, and any other hardware that might show, for continuity.

IIIII accentuate windows with decorative rods and rings IIII

BELOW An ordinary window is transformed into a focal point when fancy finial-style brackets are used to create an upswept swag valance.

RIGHT Curtain clips and rod in satin chrome are a trendy way to update the look of window treatments.

OPPOSITE TOP LEFT An unassuming white-painted wooden rod plays up the pattern of checked-ribbon curtain ties.

OPPOSITE TOP RIGHT Glass-ball finials accentuate this attractive design.

OPPOSITE BOTTOM Heavy panels need sturdy hardware like this wooden pole, which has been stained a deep tone to coordinate with the room's furniture. Gold accents add glitz.

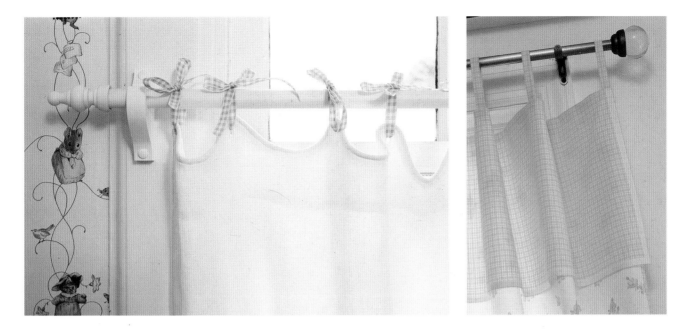

walls

Walls are the largest structural element in a room and, as such, have the potential to make the most impact on your decor. And while there are two standard choices for decorating walls—wallcovering and paint—the assortment of options and versatility regarding each one are almost endless today. Wallcoverings can include papers featuring small motifs, oversized murals, natural textures, and faux finishes. When you want to add drama to a room but prefer furniture with a more neutral, timeless sensibility, cover your walls with interesting wallpaper. Don't overlook painted or stained wood paneling as an option, especially for traditional-style interiors.

Paint is the most common type of wall treatment. It is easy to apply, simple to change, the least expensive, and quickest option for transforming the look of a room. Apply a neutral color to form a demure background when furniture and accessories are fussy. Paint the trim or an accent wall in a contrasting color, or apply a faux finish to boost the style quotient in a room that may have little architectural interest.

Don't forget the ceiling. Paint it decorator white or the very palest blue to visually heighten the room. Install decorative panels that resemble vintage tin ceilings or embossed paper or tiles. Add a wallpaper border on the wall just below the ceiling to draw the eye upward. Or for a bold design move, paint a mural on the ceiling.

TOP Some people shy away from painting walls with a dark hue, but doing so lends warmth to a room and makes accessories and trimwork pop.

LEFT Inspired by the natural light, an amber-tinted glaze has been applied to the walls with a rag to simulate texture.

OPPOSITE Formality and restraint have guided the decoration of this sitting room, hence the choice for subtle, muted gold walls. A hand-painted accent adds a rich touch. It is repeated in the painted medallion that graces the ceiling and draws attention to the chandelier.

ABOVE LEFT An ordinary hallway is transformed by a painted rusticated stone wall.

ABOVE RIGHT The walls in this bedroom were painted with a comb to create a strié effect. White painted wood-work looks crisp against the cool blue.

RIGHT Period wallpaper coupled with dark painted trim instantly "ages" a library and adds refinement to the decor.

▌▌▌ wrap a room with color, contrast, texture, and pattern ▌▌▌▌▌

ABOVE A textured vinyl wallcovering has the look of a natural weave, but it is far less delicate.

▌

FAR LEFT Color-washed walls in the French-brush technique command attention.

▌

LEFT Tone-on-tone wallpaper subtly introduces pattern to the walls here.

LEFT AND ABOVE Birds and vines painted freehand across the walls of this sun porch bring a sense of the outdoors inside.

LEFT AND BELOW Fresh formality is achieved when copies of antique prints are decoupaged to the wall to match the framed prints. This age-old technique involves gluing paper images to a surface and applying a clear top coat.

painted effects

Sponging, stenciling, trompe l'oeil, stippling, and other painted effects are enjoying a renaissance of popularity because they offer an easy and inexpensive way to add personality to a room. Some, such as trompe l'oeil, require the expertise of a professional artist. Others are easier to apply. If you want to try your hand at one, practice on a board first. Even the simplest finish may require instruction, which is easy to find in a related book, *Decorative Painting and Faux Finishes*. **Sponging** produces a highly textured surface with great visual depth, a real benefit when the wall has imperfections to hide. The technique involves two colors. One is used as a base coat. The other is dabbed on top with a sponge to create a mottled, textured look. **Ragging on** and **ragging off** are similar to sponging, except a wadded, lint-free cloth is used. **Combing** and **dragging** involve dragging a comb, brush, or other tool over a freshly applied layer of paint to reveal a complementary background color. **Stenciling** is achieved by using a pre-cut stencil to create a stylized motif. And **trompe l'oeil** is a sophisticated form of painting that appears to be real, hence its translation, "fool the eye."

ABOVE AND RIGHT A master bathroom uses texture to delineate between various all-white surfaces. One of the more interesting is the crackled paneling, produced with a technique that ages a surface to resemble the dried, crackled quality of paint in old houses.

a wall is a blank canvas for a mural

LEFT This realistic garden scene is a charming backdrop in a sunroom. The accessories, a bistro-style table and chairs, enhance the outdoor mood.

TOP, MIDDLE, AND RIGHT Garden-style vignettes set against a painted blue sky infuse the rest of the room with additional color. This is one way to have spring last all year.

floors

Although floors are underfoot, they don't go unnoticed, so they should hardly be an after-thought. Of all surfaces, floors take the most abuse and therefore must be durable while retaining their attractive looks. Such a crucial design element, therefore, deserves careful consideration. The right flooring material and covering influences and enhances the overall color scheme and look of an interior. The wrong choice may be hard to live with because it may be uncomfortable, unattractive, or simply unable to hold up to traffic.

Like paint choices, there are lots of options for flooring: wood, laminate, carpet, tile, vinyl, stone, and even linoleum, which has been recently reintroduced into the market. Because flooring can be expensive to change, it is prudent to base your decision not only on looks but durability and care requirements. For example, you might like the stark, modern appearance of an all-white carpet, but it's impractical, especially if you have children or pets. In that case, you will need something that won't show dirt and will wear better. If you like the warmth of wood but can't afford a real wood floor, look at the wood laminates, which come cheaper, don't require much care, but have a limited life span of about 15 years. Other factors to ponder include a room's function and how the material you choose works with your design scheme. If there's a lot of pattern on the walls or in the fabric, keep the floor simple. If the reverse is true, enliven a plain room with a bold print or add texture with a cut or nubby pile carpet.

As you review flooring options, keep in mind that some can be mixed and matched for an interesting and creative design variation that combines expensive and inexpensive materials. Wood planks, for example, might be bordered by ceramic-tile strips, or top-quality stone edging might provide an unusual framework for a relatively inexpensive run of carpeting.

RIGHT The owners of this house used a bold tri-tone, diamond-pattern stain to dress up older wood floors.

creativity underfoot

LEFT For protection, painted or stenciled designs should be applied before the final top coat.

ABOVE The wood-laminate floor looks like authentic pine planks, but it can be used in moist areas like this bathroom.

BELOW A rustic real-wood floor looks right at home in front of the stone fireplace. Wood is hard wearing, but it requires periodic refinishing.

bright idea
freehand style

This scroll design is a simple motif that can be applied freehand around the edge of a wood floor or to create a frame somewhere in the middle. It defines the space and eliminates the need for a decorative rug. Turn to other themes in the room for pattern inspiration.

wood—**r**ustic or **r**efined

Wood floors are a perennial flooring favorite, in part because of their durability but also because of their warmth. Wood can be factory- or custom-stained and is available in strips from 1 to 10 inches wide, a choice that you will make depending on your budget and taste. Parquet flooring, which has intricate pieces of wood laid in various patterns, is another option. Both types of wood flooring can be purchased as prefinished blocks, a reasonable alternative to their custom counterparts.

The different types of wood used for flooring are vast, and their cost varies widely according to the type, grade, and design. Softwoods, such as pine and fir, are often used to make simple tongue-and-groove floorboards. These floors are less expensive than hardwoods but also less durable. Softwoods are not suitable for high-traffic areas, for rooms with heavy furniture, or for kitchens or dining rooms where chairs or other furniture are constantly scooted across the surface. Hardwoods such as maple, birch, oak, and ash are far less likely to mar with normal use. A hardwood floor is not indestructible; however, it will stand up to demanding everyday use.

Wood is graded by its color, grain, and imperfections. The highest quality is known as clear, followed by select, No. 1 common, No. 2 common, and cabin grade. Stains for wood floors may be used to enhance the natural color of the wood or to lighten or darken the natural color according to preference. Light stains look best with informal styles and create a feeling of openness to make a small room feel larger. Darker stains feel more intimate and reduce the visual vastness of a large space. They also look appropriate in a formal decor.

ceramic and stone

Like wood, ceramic and stone have long been used as flooring materials. With so many modern renditions, it is easy to use these finishes in any room. The beauty of both of these materials is that tiles can be mixed and matched to create intricate patterns that are virtually indestructible. They also offer a richness of color and are easy to maintain. However, both are cold underfoot, noisy when walked on in hard-soled shoes, and not at all resilient.

Ceramic tile is actually fired clay and is an excellent choice for areas subject to heavy traffic and in rooms where resistance to moisture and stains is needed. Tile comes in a variety of sizes, from 1-inch-square mosaic versions to large 16 x 16-inch squares. When finished, tile can be shiny or matte, with a smooth or rippled surface texture. Glazed tiles have a hard, typically colored surface that is applied during the firing process. Unglazed tiles, such as Saltillo or quarry tiles, have a matte finish, are porous, and should be sealed to prevent staining. Make sure that any tile that is installed on the floor is specified for that purpose. Highly glazed tiles, for example, are too slippery for application outdoors.

Stone has a rustic irregularity and random color variations that make its natural beauty unparalleled, even by the most expert of faux finishes. Stone's unique traits come with a price, as this material is at least twice the cost of ceramic and often several times more. Marble, granite, random-cut fieldstone, slate, brick, terrazzo, or limestone are all beautiful and can add value and elegance to your home. But if they are too costly, consider the versatility and design possibilities offered by concrete. No longer drab gray, new color stains and inlaid designs in concrete are dynamic.

floors can be cool in many ways

LEFT Large squares of charcoal-gray slate look elegant yet understated in this setting. They coordinate beautifully with the green-blue glass mosaic tiles on the wall behind the tub.

OPPOSITE BOTTOM LEFT Even though it has been used in home interiors for centuries, marble has a fresh, fashionable look today.

OPPOSITE BOTTOM RIGHT Pretty, opalescent umber-colored glass insets jazz up these earthy porcelain tiles.

bright idea

stone at home

In an open plan, flooring that can smoothly transition from one room to the next is especially important. Classic stone in a neutral color makes a grand appearance in this foyer yet also blends subtly into the living room.

ABOVE Create interest by layering various sizes, colors, and types of tile. Slate, ceramic, and glass tiles were used in this composition.

soften the space IIIIIIIIIIIIIII

bright idea

canvas gets the vote

Painted canvas floorcloths are a less-expensive alternative to intricate rugs, and the technique is simple enough for novices to try. Once the painted area is dry, several coats of polyurethane are brushed on for protection.

ABOVE Artwork underfoot—that's the beauty of a painted floorcloth. Paint it to match other elements in the room. If freehand isn't your style, try a stencil.

TOP RIGHT Carpet runners in a neutral color keep small areas, such as this landing and narrow hallway, open and bright.

RIGHT A colorful, bold floral runner is a great way to perk up a long narrow corridor.

carpets and rugs

Carpets are a popular choice for flooring. They bring a softness to floors that can't be simulated by other flooring materials. Carpeting is the term used for large stretches of flooring that is usually installed wall to wall. Rugs are considered soft floor coverings. They are not wall-to-wall and can be used over another finished flooring surface. Both, however, are constructed from the same types of materials.

Choosing a carpet or rug is a big decision, in part because of the differences in fiber composition, construction, color, texture, and cost. Carpeting can be made from natural wool, synthetic fibers, or blends of wool and synthetics. Rugs are also fashioned from these materials, but can also be made from cotton or plant materials such as hemp, jute, sisal, or grasses.

Woven carpet is the most durable of construction methods, while flocking, a process that bonds the end of short fibers to a backing, is the least. The durability of tufting, needle punched, and knitted carpets fall somewhere in between.

The way a carpet or rug feels is determined by its "pile," or surface. A loop pile leaves loops intact when the carpet is connected to a backing. Cut pile has cut loops. Tip-sheared carpets are a combination of cut and uncut loops. Berber carpeting is short-loop-pile carpeting, while shag carpeting features long-cut pile.

What's right for your application? Look for something that's wear- and stain-resistant if you have kids, pets, or an accident-prone adult in the house. Make sure the stain protection is applied at the mill if you want it to be permanent. Otherwise, every time you clean the carpet or spot-treat it, you will have to reapply stain protection.

TOP RIGHT Neutral wall-to-wall carpet is an obvious choice in a modern living room, especially if you like to lounge on the floor.

RIGHT A colorful striped rug plays up the strong lines of the bookcases, windows, and coffered ceiling in this study, and it keeps the look informal.

The rooms where your family and friends congregate should possess an atmosphere that is both comfortable and inviting. Yet equally important is the practicality of those rooms. Gathering places often serve many purposes and, therefore, must be able to look good while serving a number of functions. For example, the family room might double as a media room, complete with computer, television, and stereo system. And a living room could serve the dual purposes of a sitting area and a dining room. This chapter focuses on creative ways that bring both form and function to your living areas.

Gathering Places

▌living rooms ▌family rooms ▌
▌dining rooms ▌

Open floor plans and multifunctional spaces suit today's relaxed lifestyle. Here, the flow between the kitchen and the dining room makes entertaining easy.

living rooms

Traditionally, living rooms have been formal spaces used only to entertain company or for spillover from large family gatherings. Today, however, homeowners often need every room in the house to accommodate their family's ever-changing needs. As a result, although living rooms might be more formal than other gathering places, they are hardly off limits. A library, children's play space, dining room, and even home office may be one of your living room's other functions.

The style of the living room is usually the foundation for the rest of the home's interior design. That's because many interior designers begin a decorating project with the living room, then repeat theme, color, or other decorative elements in other parts of the house. If your house also has a family room, your living room may be the more formal of the two, but that doesn't mean it has to be uncomfortable and stuffy. Indeed, a room with a pleasant ambiance and comfortable seating—no matter what the style—will make guests feel at home and family members relaxed. If the living room is the only place for gathering, be sure to showcase items such as family mementoes or pictures to make the space personal.

Whether you normally reserve the living room for entertaining or use it everyday, furnish it comfortably. Keep furniture away from the walls and cluster pieces together to create intimate conversation areas, television viewing spaces, or even a quiet corner for reading. If needed, use screens, rugs, or bookcases to create distinct separations between areas.

OPPOSITE Furniture groupings define spaces within a large room. The sofa and loveseat form a conversation area, while the armoire houses a corner bar.

ABOVE Choose furniture with dual functions. An ottoman works as a coffee table or extra seating. A console behind the loveseat provides storage and a flat surface for putting down a glass or a tray of canapés when company calls.

RIGHT Avoid the urge to decorate each space differently in a large room. Instead, arrange furniture as needed for function, but unify the space with coordinating fabrics in the curtains and toss pillows, a rug that anchors a seating arrangement, and the overall color scheme.

OPPOSITE A mirrored screen in the corner helps to visually amplify the room's size by reflecting light and color. Small-scale chairs and leather ottomans can be easily rearranged for large parties or small gatherings.

LEFT A grand piano, the largest and darkest object in the room, is an obvious focal point.

BELOW An aisle created behind the chairs allows people to meander to an adjacent sunroom when the living room becomes crowded.

▌▌ function, form, and focus ▐▐▐▐▐▐▐▐▐▐▐▐▐▐▐▐▐▐▐▐▐▐▐▐▐▐▐▐▐▐▐▐▐

bright idea
flexible is sensible

Oversize furniture can crowd small rooms. Instead, opt for multiples of slim, clean-lined pieces, a design trick that creates more impact than one large item and results in a modern, coordinated look.

5 beauty tips for the living room

Decorating should hardly be daunting. Try these tried-and-true tips—the same ones professionals use—to boost the style quotient in your living room.

▌ **Create Conversation Stations.** Bring furniture in from walls to create cozy sitting areas that invite conversation. When furniture is spread too far apart, it creates an empty, dead zone in the center of the room.

▌ **Anchor the Arrangement.** When a room does double duty, make each space distinct by anchoring it with a rug. This gives you a perimeter to define each area, brings order to your arrangements, and keeps furniture from being disconnected.

▌ **Curb Clutter.** Group like objects such as collections and picture frames, provide storage for media items, and toss magazines. Doing so will streamline your decor and make the space appear—and function—as if it's larger.

▌ **Provide Continuity with Color.** Resist the urge to use different colors throughout the house. Establish continuity with one or two dominant colors; then accessorize with complementary colors.

▌ **Read between the Lines.** Every room can be reduced to lines. To keep your decorating scheme from appearing choppy and mismatched, arrange furniture at one height and artwork at another. Unify odd shaped windows by hanging curtains from the same line or point on the wall.

OPPOSITE AND ABOVE Each seating area in a large living room has its own personality, even though the color choices are similar for each. The yellow couch in the formal sitting area (opposite) is from the same color family as the chairs in the casual seating arrangement (above). Complementary reds and greens are found in both. Keeping furniture at the same height has a unifying effect on the seating arrangements. Also note how the furniture is placed along the lines created by the coffered ceiling.

LEFT When not in use, electronic equipment and accessories hide behind custom drawers and cabinets. Shelves on either side also provide storage.

OPPOSITE TOP Rooms that open to each other can share focal points, and sightlines become very important. This living room looks straight into the dining room, where the chandelier is hard to ignore.
▮

OPPOSITE BOTTOM In the same home, this view is from the dining room's perspective. The tall armoire draws the eye into the adjacent space.
▮

BELOW Architectural features are often focal points—a massive fireplace, for example. The staircase and cubicle grid underneath it command attention, as well.
▮

BELOW RIGHT The view into the room and through French doors is inviting.

focal points & sightlines

Every room benefits from a focal point. When you walk into a room, your eye bounces from place to place until it finds somewhere to rest. If you don't have a focal point, your eye continues moving and your decor appears cluttered and busy.

Some focal points are obvious. A fireplace and built-in cabinetry or a large picture window can assume the role. However, a main area of focus can also be created with a dramatic piece of furniture, such as a bookcase or wall unit, a large coffee table, an eye-catching painting, a stunning light fixture, or even accent or decorative lighting itself.

After establishing a focal point, ensure that the room offers unobstructed sightlines. These are the lines of sight into or out from a room or from the viewer to an object. Observe what you see when you look through a doorway. Also, when you are arranging furniture and accessories, it is essential that you leave a clear viewing path. A room filled with too many accessories, mismatched furniture, and obstructive lighting will appear incongruous and without focus. Sightlines actually draw the eye into a setting and allow it to rest on the focal point.

The name says it all: a family room is where families spend time relaxing together. Foremost, a family room should reflect your family's lifestyle. A professional couple's living space will vary drastically from a room designed around a family with

family rooms

young children. The same is true for personality. A room for families who entertain will look totally different from a room for families who turn to the family room as a retreat.

Special consideration should be given to great rooms—family rooms and kitchens contained in one open space. Coordinate them, but create visual separation, too. This can be achieved by arranging the family-room furniture to face away from the kitchen or by alternating materials. Use ceramic tile on the kitchen floor and hardwood in the family room, or use hardwood throughout the space, clustering family-room furniture around area rugs.

Color is always an important choice for living areas. Look to upholstered furniture—the hardest decorating element to change—to inspire your choices for walls, curtains, and accessories. Furniture selection is key. Seating should be comfortable and durable, especially when it takes daily use. Tables should be conveniently placed next to, in front of, or behind seating pieces for easy access. The right lighting is a must. Provide proper fixtures for task lighting in areas where you will read, play games, or do the crossword puzzle. But don't forget to install dimmers on any general light sources so you can adjust the light level for TV viewing. Always include one or two storage pieces.

OPPOSITE TOP The elegant furnishings and ornate accessories in this family room are downplayed by the warm, inviting color scheme and casual arrangement of furniture.

OPPOSITE BOTTOM Family rooms are perfect for letting your personality shine. Here, a stone fireplace becomes an informal backdrop for several layers of accessories—a look that might feel cluttered in a formal living room but one that has a cozy, lived-in appeal in a family room. Cabinets to hide electronics and media flank the fireplace.

ABOVE The larger the family room, the better. The extra space will allow you to create separate entertainment areas for your family's activities, from playing pool and working puzzles to watching TV or reading.

||||| inconspicuous placement for electronics | | | | | | | | | | | | | | |

TOP LEFT A handsome backdrop for a Craftsman-style family room, paneled cabinetry is configured to hold and hide a TV and other media equipment.

ABOVE On the opposite side of the room, the fireplace is the focal point, but the television can still be viewed from the seating area surrounding it.

RIGHT In another family room, placing the TV in built-in cabinetry eliminates the need for freestanding furniture and keeps it from becoming the focus of the room.

bright idea

open and shut Case

A false panel hides the TV niche above a fireplace. When not in use, a painting that hangs on the panel adds to the realism of the disguise and complements the fireplace.

fireplaces

Once a necessity in the home, the fireplace has evolved into a stylish amenity. Indeed, any room graced with a fireplace, whether it is the living room, a bedroom, or the kitchen, gains a dominant and commanding focal point. Old or new, fireplaces add warmth.

A stark, minimalist look can be achieved if your fireplace consists of nothing more than the rectangular firebox and hearth. The clean lines don't interfere with other design aspects in the room, and there is no mantelshelf above to dress with busy displays. If you prefer a more traditional look, adding a mantel can dress up the space. Some mantels are simply a horizontal plank shelf above the fireplace opening. Others feature detailed woodwork and have fancy jambs for support that frame the sides of the fireplace.

Fireplaces are made from a variety of materials, with brick as the most common. Stone, tile, marble, concrete, and stucco are other options and are usually chosen in accordance with the style of your home. All the materials are durable, and all can be applied to produce unlimited designs and finishes.

If you have a working wood-burning fireplace that you frequently use, keep accessories such as pokers, shovels, and wood bins within reach for convenience. If you rarely light a fire or during the warm months when a fire is unnecessary, stack wood inside for effect or use the firebox as an unusual place to display items like baskets, plants, dried flowers, and candles.

ABOVE A stacked stone fireplace needs a hefty shelf mantel to balance the massive firebox below.

RIGHT Marble is a classic choice for fireplace surrounds. The wood surround matches the flanking cabinetry.

BELOW In this family room, a flat-screen TV is installed over the raised stone fireplace.

open floor plans visually and literally create space

ABOVE LEFT In a large open layout, a billiards table defines the "game room."

ABOVE RIGHT Upholstered seating creates the "boundary" for the TV room.

OPPOSITE In a great room, which has lots of space for various activities, the kitchen provides an important anchor. The large curved kitchen island and breakfast bar here almost completely hide the work surfaces—a plus in an open layout of shared spaces.

RIGHT Floor-to-ceiling doors in another part of the same great room mentioned above extend the living space to a large covered outdoor deck during warm-weather months.

BELOW Wide, uninterrupted passages between interior and exterior areas maximize space. Still in the same room, the formal dining room is just steps beyond the other gathering spots.

bright idea

good trick

Use artwork to create the illusion of windows in a room such as a basement or attic. To maximize the illusion (not done here), keep the frame size consistent and hang them all at the same level where windows might appear on the wall.

ABOVE Cheerful and upbeat, a colorful pastel palette enlivens a basement family room.

LEFT A billiards room requires empty space around the table, but you can use the walls and displays on narrow shelving to add personality to the room's decor.

OPPOSITE Painting walls black is a bold move, but the result is striking—and effective. Like movie theaters, which often have dark walls, black decreases glare and enhances viewing.

fun and games

All too often, a room reserved for fun and games is a decorating afterthought. Yet because this is where your passions play out, it is important that it should be uplifting and conducive to the types of activities that you enjoy. Begin with the activity itself. Painters need white space surrounding their easel, a floor that can be messed up or that is easy to clean, and lots of natural light. Sports enthusiasts enjoy comfortable seating for watching games, tables to hold drinks and snacks, and an entertainment center that brings the game front and center. Crafters require a solid work surface, bulletin boards to post ideas and tear sheets for future projects, and shelving, baskets, and bins (preferably clear) to stash supplies. If you focus on the activity, the design needs will become evident.

If you have a budget for decorating, plan beforehand for furnishings, lighting, storage, and any special equipment you might need, such as a mat for an in-home gym. A well-conceived plan will keep this room from becoming a catch-all for overflow from other rooms. Likewise, if you are using furniture and accessories you have on hand, look for a common element in each that will tie the room together. A color or motif is a good place to start. If your existing items are mismatched, inexpensive slipcovers, a fresh coat of paint, and even a disciplined editing of accessories updates and refreshes tired pieces or ones that you pick up at a yard sale.

media **r**oom **t**ips

Give your local movie theater a run for its money by creating an in-home media room with all the electronic bells and whistles.

❚ Start with the equipment. Don't buy a TV that's too big for your space. Speakers placed throughout the room, an AM/FM receiver, and DVD player are the key equipment you'll need for surround sound.

❚ Comfortable seating is essential. Check into special designs created just for movie viewing at home.

❚ Control the light. Install window treatments that block sunlight and glare.

❚ Keep it cool. Control the temperature; electronics can heat up a room.

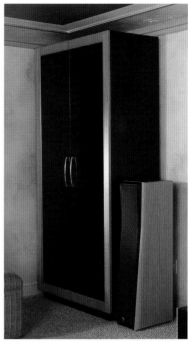

ABOVE A sleek armoire disguises unsightly cords, gaming equipment, and stacks of CDs and DVDs.

OPPOSITE TOP An oversized sofa beckons guests to sink right in. It is arranged so that the media center is the focus.

OPPOSITE BOTTOM Fully lined Roman shades are easy to open and close to block light.

ABOVE LEFT With upholstered stools and a roomy countertop, a custom-made bar is ideal for serving cocktails and kicking back to watch the game.

RIGHT The front-projection TV screen drops down for viewing from the bar or the sofa. The projector is mounted on the ceiling.

bright idea

at your service

Turn to specialty stores for an array of unique merchandise and accessories to make your media room functional and fashionable. Chairs such as these are as comfortable as traditional recliners but come complete with cup holders and built-in trays.

ABOVE If your room is strictly for viewing, forego convention and place furniture, in true theater fashion, on elevated platforms. Include wall-to-wall carpeting for sound absorption.

LEFT Today's furniture options include all kinds of nifty accessories for ease in viewing, storage, and convenience. This example is a slide-out bin to hold DVDs.

RIGHT Pull-out drawers in an armoire will save you hours of time searching in the back for misplaced CDs and DVDs. Some storage units come with pullout drawers built-in. For others, there are kits you can purchase and install yourself.

BELOW A sectional sofa gives everyone a front-row seat and creates a cozy viewing area perfect for hanging out with friends. An ottoman in the center can serve as a footstool or table. The semi-custom cabinetry houses all of the TV and sound equipment and accessories.

5

Style extends to the kitchen because so much living and entertaining takes place there today. Even though this room has to be practical, it should look good and feel inviting, too. It's not difficult to put your personal stamp on the kitchen, as well. The style that's right will probably harmonize with the design of the rest of your house. Whether your taste is for things formal or casual, traditional or contemporary, you can find cabinets, countertops, wall treatments, flooring, and decorative details that will pull your look together without sacrificing function.

Kitchens

I traditional I country I contemporary I cabinets I wall treatments I flooring I ceilings I countertops I

This cheerful and chic kitchen is designed to function as both a place to work for a serious cook and a casual gathering spot for family and friends.

One of the reasons for the popularity of traditional style is its timelessness and the fact that it is unaffected by design trends that come and go. For a traditional-style kitchen, where the ambiance is elegant, gracious, and just a little bit formal, cabinets are most commonly crafted of rich, gleaming woods, usually cherry or mahogany or any wood stained to resemble them. Ivory- or white-painted cabinets are another frequent choice, but the key to the cabinets is a rich, glossy finish and the look of fine furniture. For the cabi-

traditional

net door style, choose a raised-panel design and such architectural details as crown moldings and other millwork. Countertops, which are typically made of a glossy, polished stone such as granite or marble—or a solid-surfacing or plastic laminate look-alike—may also feature rich details such as bull-nose or beveled edges. Choosing countertop colors of deep green, dark gray, or black will add richness, as will wood floors or a classic black-and-white checkerboard pattern in ceramic tile or vinyl. Reproduction-style hardware and light fixtures will add the perfect details.

LEFT Featuring formality on the light side, this kitchen in the American traditional style combines light wood, granite counters in a pale shade, and lots of sunlight. The chandelier strikes the right formal note.

OPPOSITE BOTTOM LEFT To maintain the traditional look, the front of the side-by-side refrigerator/ freezer is disguised by full overlay panels that are custom-made to match the cabinetry.

BELOW LEFT Curved-back chairs and a china cabinet with fine-furniture detailing grace the eating area. Muntins on the patio doors are a nice touch.

RIGHT This design relies on a crisp black-and-white tiled backsplash and honey-toned cabinets for its all-American appeal.

bright idea

coffee station

This little corner is reserved for an espresso machine. The granite countertop is stylish and practical as a heat-resistant surface.

southern accents

ABOVE A generous island welcomes family and friends to gather in front of the cooking hearth.

LEFT Drawers and cupboards in a wide variety of sizes answer every possible storage need.

BELOW This room mixes plain Southern pine cabinets with fancy details: crown molding, turned legs, and roped and fluted pilasters.

bright idea
distinct design
Crown moldings and other millwork are key to the gracious look of traditional kitchens.

|| french flavor || || || || || || || || || || || || || || || || || || || || || || || || ||

ABOVE Formal cabinetry with handsome detailing and brass hardware defines this traditional kitchen. The focal point is a bay window that frames views of a pretty garden. A hammered-copper front on the exposed-apron sink adds French-style texture.

LEFT A mélange of elements contributes to the French traditional look here—white-painted cabinetry, colorful tiles, rattan dining stools, and copper accents throughout.

a take on tuscany

TOP Natural materials and earthy colors reveal the Tuscan inspiration for this design.

ABOVE LEFT An unfitted look is also essential to the style. Here, sturdy farmhouse-like cabinets and furniture are deliberately mismatched, then done up in different colors.

ABOVE RIGHT The dining area glows with color and texture—a wood ceiling, tile floor, olive-color walls, and deep-red chairs. A wrought-iron chandelier tops it off beautifully.

RIGHT The cabinets are slightly distressed for an appropriately rustic look.

OPPOSITE FAR RIGHT Arches and other classical motifs enhance the Old World atmosphere of the room. A huge island provides supplemental storage.

timeless customs

What could be more European than a thick and frothy cappuccino? And what could be more appropriate in an Old World-inspired kitchen than a coffee station? The one pictured here has been created inside a bank of cabinets with slide-in doors. But aside from an espresso machine, what other elements go into creating what we call Old World style? The look is actually a mix of French and Italian with a little Greek and Roman classicism thrown into it, too. Nothing should look shiny or new. The overall effect is comfortable with obvious signs of wear and tear. Richness in color, material, and texture is also key—rugged limestone or tumbled marble; ceramic tile; mellow woods; and disparate elements that seem to have been lovingly added piece by piece over time.

Some kitchen designers and other experts in the field theorize that we love the country look because it recalls the warmth of Grandma's kitchen, conjures up romantic notions of the keeping rooms of old, or simply links us to what we believe was a simpler, gentler time. Whatever the reason, this is an extremely popular style, and opportunity for personal expression abounds. Informal and relaxed, country is a good choice for a casual lifestyle; and because the look of wear and tear is desirable, it suits busy families and active kitchens, too. Build your country kitchen around wood cabinets in a natural stain, a pickled or bleached finish, or a cheerful paint color. Neither elegance nor sleekness is the goal; so mismatched cabinets, freestanding unfitted pieces, or open shelves filled with dishes are also appropriate. Wood floors are ideal but homey patterns in vinyl or tile would also work. Almost anything goes for countertops, but especially something that's earthy —a rustic stone or tile, for example.

country

There are many offshoots of this basic look— English country, cottage, Victorian, and Arts and Crafts, to name a few. If you're the country-kitchen type, one of these variations is sure to please you. Shown here is another variation on the theme, the new look of American country, a slightly more sophisticated style with sleeker lines and fewer accessories than its predecessor.

RIGHT This design takes country to a sophisticated new level. Cabinets with sleeker lines and elegant granite counters intermingle here with the usual down-home charm and informal mix of woods and hardware.

TOP In keeping with the heart-of-the-home country philosophy, the kitchen is open to an inviting family dining area.

ABOVE Even a sleek version of country allows for personal expression. Cookbooks, family photos, and framed prints occupy a corner of the room.

RIGHT An interior window opens into an enclosed porch and is used as a pass-through for informal meals.

country style has many

OPPOSITE TOP For those who love log cabins and the outdoor life, this style is a great choice for the kitchen. The warm tones of the wood cabinets make it cozy, and the arched window frames a woodsy view. Note the distinctive Arts and Crafts details on the window and hanging lamp.

OPPOSITE BOTTOM LEFT A massive fieldstone arch encloses the cooking center and creates the aura of a hunting lodge in the woods.

OPPOSITE BOTTOM RIGHT In addition to providing a work surface and extra storage, the sturdy, rustic island is an important decorative element. Wood flooring is a comfortable choice for underfoot.

LEFT Extensive use of mellow wood is the key to this cabin-style kitchen. The butcher-block island holds a handy second sink that allows two people to work on food preparation together.

creating the cottage style

An amalgam of English country and Victorian bungalow, the cottage kitchen ranges from rustic to refined. An all-white scheme puts the room shown here in the refined category, but all the key elements of the overall style are represented—painted wood cabinets, beadboard backsplash, plate racks, and glass-fronted cabinets. Other versions of a cottage kitchen might include colorful, mismatched, and slightly worn-looking cabinets and vintage furniture and accessories.

looks, from rustic cabin to cozy cottage IIIIIIIIIIIIIIIIIIII

LEFT Simple cabinets with a hand-made appearance and exposed beams and rafters contribute to the rural air of this farmhouse kitchen.

BELOW LEFT Period-style faucets resemble the pumps that once brought water to kitchen sinks. These days they're handy for filling tall pots.

BELOW RIGHT Essential to the look is a kitchen table where people gather. The island serves this purpose and doubles as a food-preparation counter.

american farmhouse versus

a lived-in look

The English country style does not derive from the great houses of the English countryside but from modest homes and bungalows that have been lived in comfortably for generations and are pleasantly cluttered. To re-create this style, choose cabinets with a patina of age and details such as plate racks, niches, and glass fronts. For floors, wood or matte-finish tile works well; countertops may be stone, solid-surfacing, or wood—any material that does not look shiny and new. The desired effect resembles an Old World kitchen, but the colors are lighter, and personal collections of English china are key.

english country

ABOVE Intricately designed cabinets are a sure sign of English country, as is the warm cream paint color that looks gently aged.

RIGHT Much of this kitchen's charm comes from the cooking hearth—a throwback to earlier times. Now it's equipped with a professional range.

RIGHT Old World style offers an interesting alternative to American country, featuring earthier colors, a stronger emphasis on stone, cabinetry that resembles unfitted pieces of antique furniture, and mellow patinas.

BELOW An alcove with a rustic-looking wooden bench and tall casement windows is an inspired Old World touch.

old world style

bright idea
the niche
A built-in shelf within the cooking hearth can be decorative or useful as a place to keep infused oils or spices handy.

OPPOSITE Details make the difference—a large arched window, Italian mosaic tiles on the back-splash, and the matte finished faucets and hard-ware all suggest another time and place.

RIGHT Wide aisles between the center island and the work zones make this warm family kitchen comfortable no matter how crowded it gets.

ABOVE
Au courant appliances and fixtures complement the kitchen's decor.

LEFT Style-wise, there's a little bit of everything from classical columns to a kitschy collection of vintage cookie jars. Mixed with a sure hand, all of the elements are harmonious.

anything goes

An eclectic kitchen is very personal. It brings together elements from different styles and eras and makes them visually cohesive. It's not easy to pull off, but this advice from designer Rick Shaver of Shaver-Melahn in New York City should help. "There must be a common thread, be it color, texture, architectural detail, even collectibles," says Shaver, who designs furniture as well as interiors. The kitchen shown here relies on architectural detail to unite its disparate elements. Another eclectic design might be held together thematically by displays of collections such as bowls, kitchen utensils, or transferware.

eclectic style mixes it up

ABOVE An imposing bank of black-painted upper cabinets is a surprising touch that works because it looks like an old china cabinet.

ABOVE RIGHT A backsplash of windows brightens the look by day; cabinet lighting takes over at night.

RIGHT Details from several styles and eras—including a mid-century kitchen set—enliven the room with a unique point of view.

ABOVE This updated contemporary-style kitchen is definitely streamlined, but not sterile. The warmth of the cabinets' wood stain, the gentle curves of the two-level island, and the rounded backs of the dining chairs soften its appearance.

LEFT True to the contemporary philosophy, the sleek cabinets are without embellishment, except for the curvilinear brushed-steel hardware and occasional glass-panel door.

OPPOSITE Countertops in natural materials, such as the granite used here, are a hallmark of contemporary kitchens. Countertop edge treatments are typically plain—either squared off or bullnosed and without bevels.

The contemporary style had its origins at the end of the nineteenth century when artists, architects, and designers rebelled against the fussy and cluttered design sensibility that prevailed throughout most of the Victorian era. Their rebellion manifested in simplicity and the use of natural materials. As the look evolved it continued to emphasize natural materials but became more and more streamlined. For a time, in the 1970s and '80s, when newly emerging technology was impacting the culture, a "high-tech" look was de rigueur in many kitchens. These designs were sleek and hard-edged; articulated in the neutral tones of stainless steel, stone, and glass; and looked almost like laboratories. Although contemporary style remains pared-down for the most part, it has warmed up considerably since then.

contemporary

The backbone of today's contemporary kitchen is frameless, flat-panel cabinetry with clean lines and simple hardware. Wood finishes, particularly maple, cherry, and birch in lighter tones, are common choices. Cabinet doors made of glass and metal—often aluminum—are popular, also, because they go well with sleek contemporary appliances. Natural surfacing materials—especially stone, tile, and concrete—or solid-surface laminate versions dominate surfaces. The Retro Modern, or Mid-Century Modern, look that can be seen in home furnishings is also influencing kitchen design. Sleek and industrial in a 1950s-70s way, it may not be for everyone, but it has a growing following.

retro modern

ABOVE Touches of the 1950s, such as curved-back plastic chairs and expanses of chartreuse, qualify this design for the retro-chic category.

LEFT A retro-style mixer in turquoise, a favorite '50s color, is an apt accessory.

RIGHT The wild color on the walls, countertop, and tile collage along the backsplash are in stark contrast to the spare contemporary cabinets and the subdued brushed metal finishes.

revisiting the **r**ecent **p**ast

A decorating style that revisits mid twentieth-century designs, Retro Modern is a manifestation of the contemporary genre. The retro chic philosophy does not suggest that you entirely re-create the look of the era; you can incorporate just a few telling details. For example, to retro-fit your kitchen with a '50s flavor, you might add diner details, such as chrome stools topped with red-leather seats or plastic-laminate countertops with the reissued boomerang pattern. Retro-style appliances are available from several manufacturers, too.

If you are fond of contemporary interiors but afraid that a kitchen designed in this clean-lined, unembellished style is doomed to look cold and clinical, think again. The contemporary kitchen has evolved over the last few decades, and the "high-tech" laboratory look is out, replaced by a warmer, friendlier version. Today's contemporary-style kitchens are still simple, spare, and equipped with the latest technology, but a new focus on wood for the cabinets and the restrained use of color as an accessory makes them as appealing and inviting as any traditional or country-style kitchen. Study the rooms on these two pages to see the influence of wood and other softening elements in state-of-the-art yet personal spaces.

warming trends

RIGHT Backsplash tiles in an earthy red-orange have a powerful warming effect in this room. Curvy chairs soften the cabinets' hard edges.

BELOW Cooktop venting equipment, which is typically encased in stainless steel, is covered in wood that matches the cabinets.

TOP In an interesting juxtaposition of styles, a clean-lined kitchen opens into a dining space with an ornate chandelier and eighteenth century-style chairs.

ABOVE Prominent grain running through the wood provides visual appeal. It also keeps the stained blue-gray cabinets from looking stark, especially next to the stainless-steel hood.

glass **a**ct

Frosted-, opaque-, textured-, wavy-, or etched-glass cabinet doors hide a multitude of sins. Behind them, cabinet contents look interesting but don't have to be neat as a pin. In addition, they don't show fingerprints as easily as clear-glass panels.

classic white

LEFT Crisp lines, polished granite countertops, and expanses of white cabinetry give this room its classic character. The mirrored back-splashes, angled island, and arched window inject visual liveliness.

TOP RIGHT In another classic-white kitchen, a stone backsplash and countertops reinforce the sleekness while adding texture. A countertop appliance provides the right dash of color required to ease the starkness.

RIGHT In this small city kitchen, light is an important factor in making the space seem larger than it is. Windows are left uncurtained in keeping with the style and to flood the room with sunlight.

ABOVE LEFT A "cabinet" for the range hood reinforces the country theme.

ABOVE Simple white cabinets set the stage for a country kitchen.

LEFT A mini butler's pantry stores china, linens, and flatware.

cabinets

Cabinets perform two important functions in the kitchen—they store and organize the necessities for cooking and they determine the design of the room. Other factors, such as countertop and flooring materials, appliances, wall and window treatments, and accessories, contribute to appearance. But cabinets are the most visible element and are therefore most responsible for the overall look.

In the kitchens of the last century, furniture was used haphazardly to hold dishes, pots and pans, and utensils, but they didn't necessarily match each other or anything else in the room. That mismatched, "unfitted" sort of look is popular again today with some homeowners, but most people prefer cabinets cut from the same design cloth to provide a unified look for the kitchen.

Once you have chosen the layout that meets your needs and the design style that reflects your taste and personality, you're ready to go cabinet shopping. Take your time. Whatever style you have settled on will be available from every major manufacturer of kitchen cabinets. Visit showrooms, look at calalogs, log on to company Web sites, and study the choices within the category you prefer. Get cost estimates, too. Armed with cost information and a rough idea of how many cabinets you'll need, you'll have a ballpark budget for the cabinet portion of your new kitchen, which according to experts, is about 40 percent of the total.

A foolproof way to figure how many storage cabinets you'll need is to empty the contents of your current ones and combine everything you want to store. Each pile of dishes, pots and pans, flatware, table linens, and cookbooks will represent one, or maybe more, of the cupboards and drawers you now require. If this method proves too disruptive and time-consuming, study your current storage situation and estimate how much more you will need, allowing for items that you'll accumulate over time.

ABOVE In this design, richly embellished cabinets furnish the flair.

BELOW Fine-furniture detailing enhances the elegant ambiance.

RIGHT Dark stain and fancy trim distinguish this china cabinet.

BELOW Unique handles are appealing.

LEFT Stately cabinets with a honey-toned stain and recessed panels make a strong design statement here.

BELOW In this space, white-painted, recessed-panel cabinets are responsible for a crisp country look. A tall corner unit topped by crown molding maximizes the farmhouse-kitchen flavor.

bright idea

details that deliver

Want to heighten visual drama in your kitchen? Add unexpected touches such as ornate architectural details, a chandelier in the work zone, or formal draperies.

ABOVE Looking for glamour in the kitchen? Choose dark, rich-looking cabinets with ornate trim; then add such touches as a chandelier, draperies, and a gilt mirror.

LEFT Panels of bird's-eye maple heighten the glamour, as does the crystal-like hardware.

Thousands of manufacturers produce attractive cabinets in a huge variety of styles, finishes, and prices. But not all of them are well-built. Don't buy kitchen cabinets just because you like the way they look. Attractive designs came in all different price ranges, and you will be able to find a style that you like whatever your budget. What is more important, however, is to scrutinize cabinets' construction details before you buy them. Beware of drawers that are nailed, glued, or just stapled together. Well-made drawers should support about 75 pounds when open. Cabinet cases should measure at least ½ inch thick all around, and interiors, including rear surfaces, should be finished. Adjustable shelves are another sign of quality. Make sure they measure at least ⅝ inch thick to prevent bowing. Look for solid hinges that don't squeak and allow doors to open fully. Some fine cabinets are made of solid wood, but a plywood box with solid-wood doors and frames also offers good structural support. Less pricey but acceptable units mix plywood supports with medium-density fiberboard doors and drawer fronts, or feature a laminate finish over high-quality, thick particleboard. Stay away from drawers made of thin particleboard. If you find a plainer style that costs less but is of good quality, you can embellish the cabinets with crown molding and different hardware.

cabinet door style choices

Door styles are strictly decorative. Styles pictured, left to right: reveal-overlay panel; frame and panel; flat panel; beaded frame and panel; square raised panel; curved raised panel; beadboard panel; and cathedral panel

OPPOSITE LEFT This cabinet sports two sure signs of high quality and careful construction—finished interiors, including the back panel, and strong hinges.

OPPOSITE RIGHT A specialized cabinet keeps spice jars handy to the cooktop. Sturdy shelves, finished to match the surrounding units, have a convenient wipe-clean surface, a feature to look for when cabinet shopping.

LEFT A mellow finish, precise design detail, and handsome brass hardware contribute to the traditional look of these kitchen cabinets.

ABOVE A recent kitchen innovation, refrigerated drawers place often-used foods in close proximity to work counters. Another convenience—the interior lights up when you open the drawer.

options

As you shop for cabinets, think about building unique areas where family and friends can come together—a home office, a place for kids to do crafts or homework, a bar, a baking zone, even an entertainment center. Inquire about cabinet options that incorporate convenient features.

RIGHT This clean-up center includes china and glassware storage, saving you trips across the room to put things away.

BELOW Positioned close to the work zone in the same kitchen, a compact home office boasts plenty of drawers, a roomy desktop, and shelves for books and collectibles.

TOP In a busy family kitchen, a microwave occupies one end of the island, out of the cook's way.

ABOVE Details such as this ornate bracket contribute a touch of elegance to the room.

LEFT Multi-purpose cabinetry includes a bar area and a niche for a TV.

ABOVE Carve out a corner in a busy kitchen for a planning desk. This one features a desktop, cabinets, and pigeonholes for organizing papers.

BELOW Conveniently situated steps away from the back door, a potting area with a porthole window would delight any gardener.

RIGHT Making the most of a few feet of wall area, this planning desk shares space with a wine cooler.

BELOW LEFT Treated with a lighter finish and door style than the rest of the cabinetry, an angled display cupboard filled with collectibles commands attention.

BELOW RIGHT A variation on a classical fluted column embellishes this corner.

framed vs. frameless construction

In framed construction, a rectangular frame outlines the cabinet box to add strength and provide a place to attach the door. The doors on frameless cabinets are laid flush over the box. No frame is visible, and hinges are often invisible as well.

Frameless A European concept that took hold here in the 1960s, frameless cabinets are a standby in contemporary kitchens. The doors fit over the entire cabinet box for a sleek and streamlined look.

Framed Cabinets with a visible frame offer richness of detail that is appropriate for traditional and country kitchens and their many design cousins.

ABOVE
Standard-sized units in this semi-custom design are laid out in an arrangement that suits the needs of the homeowners.

RIGHT Another way to create an individual look—use the same basic cabinet style but vary finishes.

There are several ways to buy cabinets for your new kitchen. *Knock-down (KD)* units go home with you the same day, and if you can install them without hiring a professional, the price is right for a tight budget. Mass-produced *stock* cabinets, issued only in standard sizes and in limited styles and finishes, are also an economical choice if quality is good. *Semi-custom* cabinets are restricted to standard sizes too, but the variety of styles, finishes, interior options, and accessories is much greater, expanding design options considerably. *Custom* cabinets, available from some cabinet companies or from local cabinetmakers, are built to your exact specifications and measurements. You'll pay a premium price, but you'll get a one-of-a kind kitchen with a personalized look and endless storage possibilities.

ABOVE This curved island was custom-created, like the rest of the cabinetry, for this high-end kitchen.

ABOVE RIGHT Other made-to-order touches to consider include glass-fronted units in a variety of sizes and specially outfitted interiors.

RIGHT This custom-made cabinetry strikes the right note in the kitchen of a late nineteenth century house.

LEFT A brick tile wall and custom range hood give this cooking center a cozy look.

BELOW LEFT A paneled exhaust hood coordinates with the walls, and the metal backsplash adds plenty of pizzazz to the cooking area.

BELOW A plaster-covered hood and the tile mural below it add Old World flavor.

OPPOSITE TOP LEFT AND RIGHT European-inspired hearth-like cooking centers have become increasingly popular, as these custom-designed alcoves illustrate.

the range hood's role in the new home hearth

BELOW LEFT AND RIGHT Examples of the redesigned "hearth" include a mantel-style range-hood cover and a clock. Both incorporate fine architectural details.

While you're focused on cabinets, appliances, and countertops for your new kitchen, don't let the walls get lost in the shuffle. The way you finish the walls will define your style and pull the design together.

Paint is the easiest and most economical wall treatment, unless you choose a decorative finish that requires a specialist. And if you want to trim the budget a little, you can do the painting yourself. Whatever color paint you decide to use, select a washable finish. And remember—ceilings don't have to be white. Painting them a lighter version of the wall color or a very pale blue is more interesting.

Wallcoverings, such as a washable vinyl, cost a little more than paint but are still quite economical to apply, especially if you do it yourself with prepasted and pretrimmed rolls: a variety of colors, patterns, and coordinating borders are available, with new ones introduced yearly.

wall treatments

Paneling, another smart surfacing choice, is the most effective way to cover up imperfections in an existing wall. The word "paneling" refers to planks or sheets used as a wall surface, and it doesn't have to look like the dreary knotty-pine you may remember from "finished" basements of the past. In fact, some paneling is quite elegant and expensive. There is a middle ground, however, with a variety of woods or wood look-alikes that can add warmth and character to your kitchen. Wainscoting, which is paneling that goes to chair-rail height, is a popular choice for country-style kitchens.

OPPOSITE A brick-red wallcovering with a subtle design enriches other warm tones in the kitchen and blends with the colors in the adjoining room, too.

ABOVE Zesty green paint looks refreshing above a half wall of white ceramic tiles.

LEFT Treated to resemble plaster, these creamy-white walls complement the elegant cabinetry and materials in this room.

how to create a rusticated stone wall

1 Draw a grid for the blocks; then apply painter's masking tape to create mortar lines. Vertical lines should be staggered and centered. Pounce on paint, twisting the brush to create a stonelike texture. Vary the coloration by applying different amounts of pressure with the brush.

2 Allow the blocks to dry, and pull off the tape. With a darker shade of paint, create shadow lines along the right or the left and the bottom of the blocks. Use an artist's brush and a broad knife as a guide. To make the shading subtle, first thin the paint with a little water.

3 When the shading lines are dry, thin full-bodied white paint, and paint the mortar lines around the blocks. Leave the shadow lines untouched except for slightly clipping their bottom corners. The final "stone wall" is now complete with an overall mottled appearance with highlights and shadows.

OPPOSITE AND BELOW A "stone" wall created with faux-painting techniques accentuates the European farmhouse flavor in this kitchen.

RIGHT A glazed finish in an open-plan kitchen and family room softens the geometric window arrangement.

BELOW RIGHT A ragged and glazed paint finish makes these walls look well worn and interesting. Their color blends beautifully with the fabrics and furniture in the room.

try a faux finish on the wall

wallpaper and paint

When it comes to kitchen wall treatments, there is only one hard-and-fast rule—use washable paints and cleanable, nonporous wallcoverings. Here are a few other decorating tips:

▌**Bold, deep paint colors** will warm up the kitchen; cool colors create calm; prints and patterns add liveliness and cheer.

▌**Not sure that a particular color** or pattern will work? Apply paint or a large wallcovering swatch to a piece of poster board; hang it on the wall; and see how you like it as the day changes. Still love it? Live with it for a week before making a decision.

▌**To establish harmony** throughout your house, choose a wall treatment that's in sync with the rooms that adjoin the kitchen.

OPPOSITE TOP LEFT Washable wallpaper in a simple medium-scale print unifies this kitchen and adjoining sitting room.

OPPOSITE TOP RIGHT A rich saturated green is an effective backdrop for a contemporary kitchen.

OPPOSITE BOTTOM Crisp and cool, this kitchen mixes bright blue wall paint with a white ceiling, cabinets, and trim.

LEFT The bold use of color—such as this terra-cotta tone—can transform a room from ordinary to warm and vibrant.

BELOW Neutral but rich, the buttery off-white paint on these walls aptly accompanies the Arts & Crafts-style cabinets.

popular **t**rimwork **p**rofiles

Greek and Roman details are a part of so many decorating styles that it's hard to find ornamental trim without some kind of classical design. The ogee shape, for instance, appears on everything from interior trimwork to exterior cornices to table edges. Here are some of the basic molding shapes and motifs that have withstood the test of time.

Torus/Astragal

Ovolo

Cavetto

Band Molding

Ogee

Scotia

Wall Molding

Quarter-Round

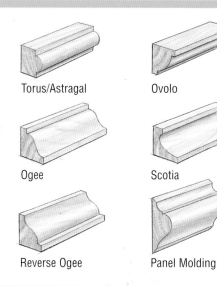

Reverse Ogee

Panel Molding

Bead-and-Reel

Bull Nose

trimwork

Architectural trim— a category that includes door and window casings, moldings, baseboards, and columns—is the crowning glory of a well-planned room, like a ribbon that puts the final beautifying touches on a gift package. It's important that you choose ornamentation that matches the style and proportions of your kitchen and the architecture of your house. Choices vary from simple to elaborate, as the drawings here illustrate. Ornate detailing works well in traditional rooms; simpler trim is more suitable for casual or contemporary settings. If you're after a really fancy effect, you may have to enlist a cabinetmaker, but check your lumberyard or home center for precut or ready-made possibilities.

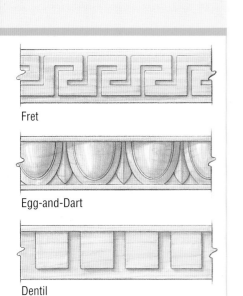

Fret

Egg-and-Dart

Dentil

OPPOSITE AND ABOVE White window and door trim, baseboards, and crown molding stand out against tomato-red wall-covering to create depth and distinction.

RIGHT Fluted columns give the passageway into this traditional kitchen a sense of importance.

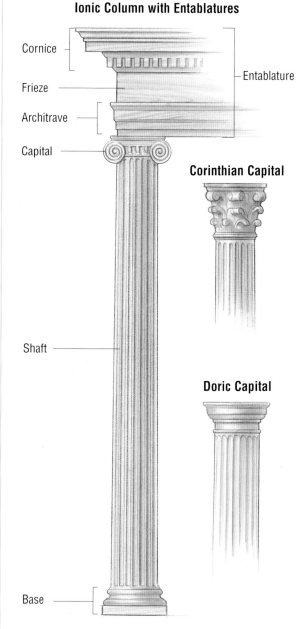

classic columns

Ionic Column with Entablatures

Cornice

Frieze

Architrave

Capital

Entablature

Shaft

Base

Corinthian Capital

Doric Capital

ABOVE LEFT AND RIGHT Whether they are original or reproductions, bull's-eye corner blocks and dentil-molding trim can add big design impact to a kitchen window.

LEFT Mitered casing distinguishes this door frame.

the difference between dull and distinctive is in

Pilaster Construction

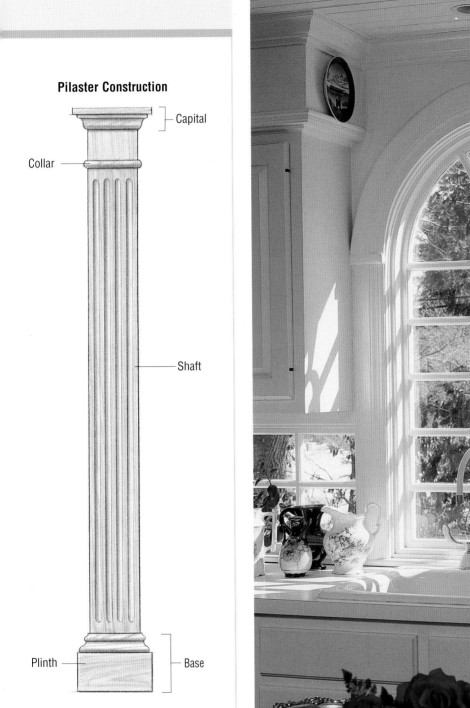

Capital

Collar

Shaft

Plinth — Base

RIGHT The focal point of this food-preparation area is a Federal-style, round-top window richly decorated with trimwork to match the cabinet trim and crown molding.

the details

door and window casings

Victorian-Style Mitered Casing

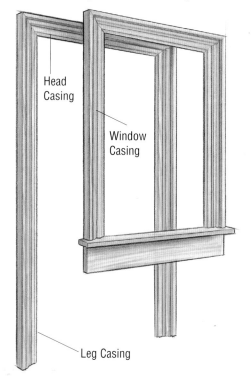

Head Casing

Window Casing

Leg Casing

Bellyband Casing with Rosette

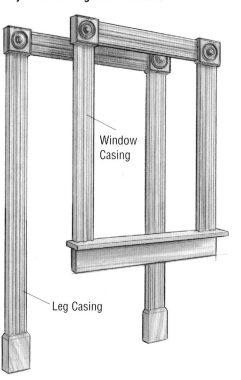

Window Casing

Leg Casing

Arts and Crafts–Style Casing

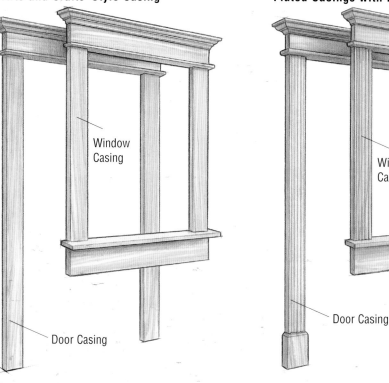

Window Casing

Door Casing

Fluted Casings with Decorative Head

Window Casing

Door Casing

OPPOSITE TOP
Low-profile clamshell moldings accentuate the otherwise undressed windows and glass doors in this contemporary room.

OPPOSITE BOTTOM LEFT AND RIGHT
Create design distinction the quick and easy way by applying wallcovering above beadboard wainscoting. Add more interest with coordinating wallcovering borders and simple chair-rail and picture-rail moldings.

bright idea

paint power

In a clean-lined room, make no-frills clamshell trim pop out pleasingly by painting it a color that contrasts with the walls.

LEFT Sheet vinyl flooring is available in many patterns, including this brick look-alike.

OPPOSITE TOP LEFT A wood floor is a natural choice for a simply stated, New England-style country kitchen.

OPPOSITE TOP RIGHT A ceramic-tile floor with diamond-shaped insets echoes the pattern in the backsplash of a classic black and white kitchen.

BELOW Linoleum, a popular material from 1900 to the 1950s, is back with updated patterns and colors.

Most of the flooring materials on the market today combine good looks with low maintenance and durability, all of which are important qualities for use in the kitchen. Because looks are important in this highly visible room, you'll want a floor that blends with the cabinets and other elements that you have chosen. When you go shopping, keep design harmony and appropriateness in mind. Wood works well with virtually any kitchen style, but stone, suitable for a contemporary room, may not be right for some traditional kitchens, and a minimalist material, such as concrete, must be used judiciously. Also, ask questions about the cleanability of the materials you like. No flooring is completely maintenance free, of course, but some require less attention than others. How much cleaning are you willing to do? The

flooring

answer to this question will help you choose. Here's another important question: how much comfort do you want underfoot? Some materials—wood, vinyl, and laminate, for instance—"give" better than others. If you'll be on your feet for long periods of time preparing complicated recipes for large numbers of people, you may want to go for a material's cushioning effect and forgo something less-forgiving, such as ceramic tile and stone. Learn about degrees of durability, too. Most modern materials are designed to stand up well to wear and tear, but if your kitchen is an especially high-traffic area, with kids and pets running through it, you'll need something that's especially tough. Select the highest quality and most durable product that you can afford and avoid "bargain" materials that you will have to replace in a few years.

The ceiling? Just paint it white—nobody notices it. If that is your attitude, you're missing a wonderful opportunity to introduce detail and warmth to your kitchen—and to inexpensively eliminate existing flaws while you're at it.

Even a simple coat of paint on the ceiling can make a difference. A light, neutral, or pastel shade of paint will be more interesting than white and will increase the feeling of light and spaciousness in the room. A medium or dark hue will create coziness and intimacy.

Ceiling tiles and panels take things a bit farther by adding texture of various kinds and becoming part of the room's design. There are many types available—some with a subtle

ceilings

textured look; others with more definite, decorative patterns. Metal tiles that re-create the look of pressed-tin ceilings common in turn-of-the-last-century rooms are also available in a variety of sizes, patterns, and finishes, including tin, copper, and brass. They are sure to make a big impact when added to a country or period-style kitchen. Your lumberyard stocks sections of tongue-and-groove and beadboard planks that resemble porch ceilings of the past, another way to bring the charm of the past to a kitchen of the present. Before you embark on a ceiling treatment, be sure that it's in keeping with the feel of your house in general and with the style of your kitchen in particular.

LEFT Wood beams, newly installed to create rustic charm, look like they've always been there.

OPPOSITE TOP New 2-ft.-square suspended plaster tiles supply instant architectural detail.

OPPOSITE BOTTOM LEFT The look of an old pressed-tin ceiling tops off this traditional kitchen.

OPPOSITE BOTTOM RIGHT Wood planks are reminiscent of the porch ceilings in older houses.

bright idea

thumbs up

Solid-surfacing pullout
shelves with dividers
are perfect for a
gardening
area.

edge treatments

Select an edge treatment for your countertop that matches the kitchen's architectural style.

Bevil

Eased Edge

Full Bull Nose

Wavy Edge

Ogee/Full Bull Nose

Large Ogee

Round-Over

Waterfall

countertops

Stone is probably the most popular countertop material today, even if it's not the most affordable. It's certainly versatile and goes with just about any decorating style. Certain types, such as granite and marble, look elegant, while slate or soapstone have more rustic appeal. Concrete, initially regarded as a countertop choice that was too sleek to look at home in any place other than a contemporary kitchen, now seems to suit all kinds of decors, especially when it's colored or inlaid with a custom design. Engineered stone and stone lookalikes in plastic laminate and solid-surfacing material offer more color variety than natural stone, but some people prefer less uniformity in the pattern. Wood counters are handsome if not always practical in a country kitchen. A wood counter will eventually show stains and scratches, but you can periodically sand out the imperfections and reseal the wood with nontoxic mineral oil. Metal, a highly sanitary material that can be safely cleaned with bleach, is a great addition to a pro-style kitchen or a minimalist design. Right now, stainless steel is the metal of choice, but copper with a baked-on, clear-coat sealer is gaining popularity. This is a look that blends beautifully into a French-country setting, but also adds warmth to a modern design.

OPPOSITE TOP A creamy white countertop coordinates well with these light wood cabinets.

OPPOSITE BOTTOM LEFT A vibrant green was selected for the countertop and pullouts in a potting bench.

LEFT A beveled edge adds an elegant detail to a traditional kitchen.

ABOVE LEFT Solid-surfacing material can imitate the look of natural stone, such as granite.

6

Some time ago people said goodbye to the boring "necessary" room and happily greeted the bath of the twenty-first century, with its limitless opportunities for comfort, design, and personal expression. Restricted only by the size of their bathrooms—and the size of their budgets—homeowners are eagerly accepting these design opportunities. Whether your decorating style preferences run to traditional, nostalgic, high tech, or drop-dead glamorous, you'll find ideas for bringing them to life in your new bath with color and other special details in the pages that follow.

Bath Style

❙ **define the look** ❙ **vanities** ❙
❙ **bathroom furniture** ❙ **walls** ❙
❙ **window treatments** ❙

All of the details, from the color palette to the trim, lighting fixtures, window treatment, art, and accessories, complement one another and enhance this bath's overall design scheme.

ALL PHOTOGRAPHS Which one of these decorating styles speaks most persuasively to you? Is it the refreshing simplicity of a cottage-style country design, **LEFT**; the rich, slightly formal graciousness of the traditional style, **BELOW**; the restrained nostalgia of the new Victorian approach, **OPPOSITE TOP**; the pared-down sleekness of the contemporary sensibility, **OPPOSITE BOTTOM LEFT**; or the ageless elegance of an Old World design, **OPPOSITE BOTTOM RIGHT**

The bath is a place where you can express your personal style. There are no rules, but styles do fall into several categories, one of which is sure to please you. In a contemporary bath, the mood is serene; fixtures, fittings, and cabinets are clean-lined and unembellished; and there is an emphasis on natural materials, such as stone, glass, and even metal. A traditional bath design relies on finely detailed cabinets in cherry or mahogany, rich, deep colors, and polished metal fittings to set a gracious and elegant tone. A country-style bath, often equipped with vintage-look tubs or pedestal lavs, is cheerier and more casual. Cottage country is casual, too, but a bit more subdued, focusing on soft pastels, faded fabrics, and gauzy curtains rather than the brighter colors of country. In both styles, however, white-painted or light cabinetry, distressed furniture, wicker pieces, baskets, and framed prints figure prominently. The key to Old World style is "old." All of the elements—mellow wood and rich shades of ochre, rust red, and olive green—should look like they've seen a lot of use but are not yet shabby. The new take on Victorian may include period-style fixtures and fittings, but the cabinets, surfaces, window treatments, and accessories will be less fussy than in the past.

define the look

contemporary modern

THIS PAGE Some of the fixtures and accessories you might choose to underscore this design theme—a sleek light fixture with a bright halogen bulb, **ABOVE LEFT;** a trendy above-counter sink with unique hand-forged fittings, **ABOVE RIGHT;** or an ultra-streamlined faucet in stainless steel, **BELOW.**

OPPOSITE This bathroom displays several of the hallmarks of contemporary modern design—a lack of embellishment, an overall streamlined look, large expanses of mirror, and the use of natural materials, such as stone, metal, and glass.

bright idea
a good fit

To be sure the faucet you like will flow into the lav you love at the right angle, buy them at the same time.

bright idea

no-fuss finish

If water spots and smudges on your faucets drive you crazy, choose a satin finish instead of a polished one.

OPPOSITE Mellow wood cabinets with the look of fine furniture set the stage for the traditional look.

LEFT To add updated elegance, you might choose faucets in a satin brass finish.

BELOW LEFT Typically used in a bedroom or hallway, wall lamps with fabric shades make gracious finishing touches in a bath.

BELOW Classic paneling and formal marble surfaces pull this look together.

traditional and timeless

country cottage casual

OPPOSITE A cousin of the enduring country style, cottage country emphasizes soft colors and a fresh, clean look.

ABOVE Vintage furniture is a cottage favorite.

RIGHT Charming old cabinets refreshed with white paint are also typical of the style.

BELOW Baskets are a staple of the style. These are beribboned and covered in linen.

bright idea

stylish storage

Use decorated or fabric-covered baskets such as these to contain the clutter of seldom-used items.

old world

OPPOSITE TOP A backdrop of stone-like ceramic tile helps to establish the Old World ambiance.

ABOVE LEFT A torchère-style wall sconce with a textured-glass shade and iron base has a vaguely medieval look, which is just right in an Old World-inspired room.

LEFT Accent tiles and border pieces have an aged look that is an essential element of the style.

ABOVE Mellow wood and ornate trim rev up the richness.

OPPOSITE A sleeker version of a period bathtub with fancy brass fittings injects Victoriana into this room, but apart from the stylized wallpaper and ornate mirror frame, the rest of the design is pure New Victorian—restrained and simple.

ABOVE RIGHT Prettily framed landscapes add interest but aren't over the top.

BELOW Handsome tilework is restricted to shades of gray stone.

new victorian

ABOVE Elegant fittings in brushed bronze complement the handsome mocha-tone marble countertop in this bathroom.

RIGHT Dramatically mounted on a mirror, this antique bronze widespread faucet flows into a matching above-counter lav.

ABOVE RIGHT Polished chrome, tried, true, and durable, is enlivened here with touches of gleaming copper.

FAR RIGHT In this unusual single-hole faucet, the chrome lever emerges from a ceramic spout that looks like a miniature water pitcher.

OPPOSITE TOP RIGHT Used together, distressed-nickel faucets and a tinted concrete basin share a soft, weathered appearance.

fixtures

Although you may not want to tackle a complete bathroom renovation, there are changes you can implement that will make both a decorative and functional splash. Today, you don't have to sacrifice panache for practicality: technology has improved along with appearance. In terms of fixtures, the easiest ones to change are the lav and the toilet. There are basic, no-nonsense versions widely available, but you may prefer to make a statement with more adventurous styles, finishes, materials, and colors. If you shop smart, you can bring home beautiful fixtures without breaking the bank.

Another option, is to simply change the faucets, which now come in myriad styles and finishes. New faucet technologies have made possible anti-scald features, flow-rate restrictors, motion-controlled models, and basic construction improvement.

Although most lavs are still made of porcelain, glazed vitreous china, or enameled cast iron, innovative shapes and colors are possible with solid surfacing, cultured stone, concrete, metal, and glass.

The latest toilets come in colors and different shapes—sculptural and modern or classic and architectural. Reproduction models recall the Victorian era. Although most residential toilets are still made of vitreous china, look for new designs made of stainless steel and accents in metal, leather, and wood.

BELOW LEFT A rugged-looking console combines a cast-concrete integral sink with a wooden base; a shelf supplies storage.

BELOW RIGHT Pedestal sinks are ideal for small spaces; this one has sufficient decking to hold soaps and toothbrushes.

BELOW LEFT Cast-concrete vessel-style lavs are partially dropped into a cast-concrete console for an ultra-contemporary look.

BELOW RIGHT Twin pedestal lavs save space in a small master bath.

RIGHT In an opulent bath, a unique porcelain console holds two sinks fitted with gleaming brass faucets.

OPPOSITE In a masterful mix of materials, a metal base supports a shiny chrome sink set into a glass counter.

the many looks of today's pedestal and console lavs

today's trends

Exotic materials. Today, a lav can be made from just about any material that will hold water—stone, concrete, hand-blown or hand-painted glass, and many kinds of metal from stainless steel and copper to luxurious pewter, silver, and even gold. The newest trend is wood, a seemingly unlikely material. But, according to manufacturers, wood lavs can be pretreated and sealed to resist warping, rotting, or buckling.

Lav furniture. Chests of drawers, marble-topped wash stands, streamlined tables, fancy metal bases—all are turning up to hold lavs and act as vanities. Transform your own furniture into a one-of-a-kind piece or check manufacturers' offerings.

Color. No longer content with white or beige, homeowners are asking for—and getting—color. Co-existing with the exotic-materials trend, the color revolution has introduced vivid reds and blues, deep greens, rich earth tones, and tropical shades such as mango, tangerine, and lime to the lav palette. In addition to solid colors, painted designs are available, usually as special orders.

Shapes. Typical round and oval designs are available in all of the hot new colors and materials, of course. But you can also purchase or custom-order rectangles, squares, long troughs, bowls, and any number of free-flowing sculpturesque configurations.

pretty in pink

Today, lavs are available in every color in the rainbow, and then some. A case in point is a curvy pink sink, looking especially interesting against a black granite counter.

OPPOSITE TOP LEFT Ornate and unique, this concrete and mosaic-tile wall-mounted sink might have come out of a centuries' old castle.

OPPOSITE TOP RIGHT With their open table-like design, console-style vanities provide the illusion of space. This one contains a stainless-steel lav and boasts a handy towel bar.

LEFT Looking more like it belongs in the bedroom, this bathroom vanity features a granite top inset with a shapely pink lav.

ABOVE RIGHT A lav set into a freestanding marble and chrome vanity is a retro mid-twentieth-century design.

RIGHT This vivid green-marble bowl can be mounted on top of or underneath a counter.

ABOVE Copper trim on the toilet tank is designed to coordinate the fixture with the undermount copper basin in the lav console.

TOP This ultra-chic toilet boasts a two-piece copper body and a wooden seat.

LEFT A French-imported two-piece toilet with hand-painted flowers and decorative trim is almost too pretty to use.

in today's bath even the toilet can be gorgeous

LEFT AND BELOW LEFT With unusual materials and clean-lined design, either of these toilets would look smashing in a modern bathroom. One toilet is completely stainless steel; the other combines stainless steel with a cherry tank panel and seat.

BELOW Based on a nineteenth-century French design, this solid-ash toilet throne features arm rests and hand-painting on the vitreous china flush cistern, the ceramic plaque, and the chain pull.

The design attention that has been focused on the bathroom for several decades has improved every aspect of it. The vanity still reigns as the major supplier of storage, but these days it looks better, stores more, and has grown taller. Because one height does not suit all people, stock vanities now range from the standard 30 inches to 36 inches high, which is easier on the back for tall people. With two vanities in the master bath, each one can be tailored to a comfortable height for its user. Vanities are also available in a couple of depths these days—18-inch-deep units free up floor space; 24-inch-deep models store more. To further improve the storage picture, the vanity is often supplemented by additional cabinets, open shelves, and freestanding furniture. Even the medicine cabinet has increased in size, functionality, and good looks.

Learn some cabinet lingo before you go shopping. For example, stock vanity cabinets, your least-expensive option, are preassembled, factory-made units that you can often take home the same day. Some of them are well made and attractive, but sizes, styles, and

vanities

finishes are limited. You'll pay a little more for a semicustom design because the variety of finishes and styles is greater, but these units are also factory made and available only in standard sizes. Custom cabinets, the most pricey option, offer the greatest design leeway because they are built to your specifications.

Available at home centers and large retail stores, stock cabinets can be inexpensive, as low as about $100 for a 36-inch-wide model. Check construction carefully before you buy—not all of them are well made. A 36-inch-wide semicustom vanity, generally available through cabinet showrooms, will cost about $300. Custom units, which are available through some manufacturers or local cabinetmakers, can be costly, but you will get a well-made product that meets specific needs.

OPPOSITE This design-savvy console is available as a stock cabinet.

ABOVE A semi-custom piece features a fine finish and ornate detailing.

LEFT AND RIGHT These custom vanities, equipped with several types of storage, were designed to meet the exact needs of the owners.

LEFT Glazed and slightly distressed to look like an antique chest of drawers, this vanity has roomy counter space, eight side drawers that are sized right for sundries, and storage underneath.

ABOVE For this bath the designer transformed an antique metalwork table into a one-of-a kind vanity with a granite countertop and an under-mounted sink.

furniture-**s**tyle **v**anities

A couple of years ago somebody—an enterprising home-owner, perhaps, or an imaginative interior designer—came upon the idea of converting an antique washstand into a bathroom vanity, complete with a sink and all the necessary plumbing. The idea spread quickly, as most good ideas do, and soon many homeowners were asking their designers and remodeling contractors to help them duplicate this look. These furniture-like vanities not only added eccentric charm and relieved the monotony of banks of cabinets that all looked alike but actually provided more storage in some cases. It wasn't long before cabinet manufacturers jumped on the band-wagon and began infusing their bath collections with trendy new vanities crafted, glazed, distressed, and ornamented with classic architectural trim to look like antique wash stands, chests of drawers, and tables. Taking the idea a little bit further, cabinet companies have now added armoires, mirrors, wall cabinets, shelves, and other storage pieces and designed them to harmonize with their furniture-like vanities. The bathroom furniture trend began with antiques, but now that it has taken hold so firmly, contemporary-looking pieces—stream-lined console tables, sleek bureaus—are also available for homeowners with a preference for modern design.

framed versus frameless designs

In framed construction, a rectangular frame outlines the cabinet box to add strength and provide a place to attach the door. The doors on frameless cabinets are laid flush over the box. No frame is visible, and hinges are often invisible as well.

▎**Frameless** A European concept that took hold here in the 1960s, frameless cabinets are a standby in contemporary-style bathrooms. The doors fit over the entire cabinet box for a sleek and streamlined look.

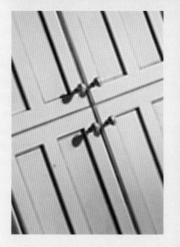

▎**Framed** Cabinets with a visible frame offer richness of detail that is appropriate for traditional and country-style bathrooms and their many design cousins.

When it comes to finishes for vanities and other bath cabinets, richness is in, starkness is out. According to interior designers and other bath specialists, there is a strong movement nowadays toward comfort in the bath, both physical and visual. Our sybaritic bathtubs and showers pamper our bodies. Now it seems, we also want pampering for our souls with a cozy, comfortable ambiance not usually associated with the bathroom.

The desire for richness and visual comfort has led to a resurgence of wood for vanities and other bath furniture, particularly warm and mellow woods such as maple, cherry, and mahogany. Glazed finishes are also on the upswing and are being used in two ways—one, as a clear coating to add depth to natural wood finishes; secondly, to create a worn yet elegant antique patina on other pieces. This new design direction also emphasizes richer, softer color. Stark white is on its way out, being replaced by warmer whites and painted finishes and laminates in off-whites such as biscuit, very pale yellows, and delicate pastels.

OPPOSITE Opulent detailing and the use of two different wood stains—one dark, one light—distinguish this vanity.

ABOVE LEFT Painted finishes in pastels and creamy hues, such as this pale buttery yellow, are making a comeback.

ABOVE Antiqued and glazed, this high-style vanity has the well-worn charm of your grandmother's bedroom furniture.

LEFT Economical and easy-to-clean, decorative laminate has been a favorite cabinet finishing material for many years.

ABOVE The look of fine old furniture characterizes this new bath cabinetry. A dark stain, marble counters, and porcelain hardware envelop the room in richness.

RIGHT With its warm wood cabinetry, brass hardware, and oversized mirror leaning against the wall, this bathroom has the aura of a gentleman's dressing room in an English manor house.

bathroom furniture

Furniture-like vanities have been such a big hit with homeowners that they have given rise to another trend—bathroom "furniture." Now, instead of restricting themselves to a single, unique-looking vanity that resembles a piece of furniture, designers are outfitting baths with several freestanding pieces, all of which look like they have been imported from the bedroom, living room, or even the kitchen. Because new bathrooms, especially master baths, tend to be large today, they can accommodate similarly scaled pieces such as bureaus, sideboards, and armoires. Besides, furniture introduces a degree of warmth and coziness not typically found in the bathroom. You can implement the look in your own bath by importing pieces from other rooms in your house or by scouring flea markets and antique stores to find a few likely candidates. If those shopping jaunts seem like too much of an effort, you can turn to cabinet manufacturers, many of whom have recently introduced custom-made, furniture-quality bath cabinets into their lines. And you'll be glad to know that this new design approach has done more than beautify the bathroom—it has also improved storage capacity. A 6-foot-tall armoire will look fabulous and will hold more items than a standard cabinet; as will the new bureau-like vanities, with their drawers of various sizes and shapes.

BELOW Frosted-glass cabinet doors, a trendy addition to bath cabinetry, enhance the mellowness of this antique finish.

RIGHT Armoires provide attractive and functional storage. Keep the contents neatly arranged and leave one door ajar for a pretty display.

matching "suites"

OPPOSITE TOP Designed to be used together, these three pieces display different details and two finishes for an informal and lively look.

OPPOSITE BOTTOM A cherry stain and architectural detailing beautify a roomy bureau-like vanity. The matching tall cabinet is for towels.

RIGHT A cherry glaze, bead detailing on the drawer and door fronts, and abundant compartments distinguish this group of cabinets.

BELOW Soft, mossy green, a new color for the bath, looks great with porcelain hardware and glass-fronted wall units.

bright idea
how suite it is

Taking its cue from the kitchen, this cabinet ensemble maximizes storage for the bath with drawers and cupboards in handy sizes.

Color is probably your greatest decorating tool. Don't be afraid of it—it also happens to be one of the easiest things to change. So why do people typically stick with a neutral palette in the bathroom? A dated color on a permanent fixture can be expensive to change because usually you have to replace the fix-

walls

ture. However, special new paints make it possible to refurbish ceramic and porcelain with a new color for a fraction of the cost of replacement.

If you still want to stick with white or beige for the tub, sink, and toilet, introduce color to the walls or with accessories. Just pick up a can of paint and see how color can transform the space in no time at all. If you don't like what you've done, just grab another can of paint and start again. It's inexpensive and easy to apply.

One of the simplest things that you can do to test out a color is to apply it to a sheet of white poster board, hang it on the wall, and live with it a few days. Look at it during the day; then wait for evening and look at it again under varying levels of artificial light. Is the color still appealing to you? What effect does it have on the space at different times of the day? Even if you're thinking about tiling a wall or installing wallpaper, pick out the dominant color, find a matching paint, and apply this simple test.

LEFT Bold blue walls combine with white fixtures, panneling, and shelving to create an appealingly crisp look.

ABOVE Even a small amount of paint makes a big impact. Here, a swath of red paint rises above the off-white paneling. The matching curtains pull it all together.

LEFT Apple-green wainscoting and mauve walls look like they belong together in this bath.

❙ ABOVE The homeowners highlighted the charms of an older bath with vibrant green walls and a bold striped Roman shade.

❙
RIGHT Bright linens can intoduce color, too.

BELOW A wallcovering with a warm, neutral background brings a couple of bonuses to this bath—a sprightly border of birdcages and a charming trompe l'oeil window.

RIGHT You can use color to draw attention to handsome features in the room. Here, weathered copper fittings stand out against the reflection of acid-green glazed walls.

OPPOSITE RIGHT The unexpected use of bright color on the walls breathes vibrant life into a period-style bath, and looks particularly refreshing against the white of the fixtures and wainscoting.

paint and **w**allpaper

While you're thinking about color for the new bathroom, consider the types of paint, wallpaper, and fabric to use. Remember, bathrooms have lots of glossy surfaces, which reflect light. Unless you want an intense effect, use low-luster paints and matte finishes.

If you are concerned about moisture, especially in a room without ducted ventilation, shop for products that have been treated with mildewcide in the manufacturing process. Bathrooms are perfect breeding grounds for mold. When moisture seeps behind wallpaper, it creates a moldy, peeling mess. Luckily, this is a problem that can be avoided because there is a wide selection of products and glues that are designed specifically for bathroom applications.

ABOVE AND RIGHT The rich wallcovering colors in this bath work with the architectural elements and furnishings to create an intriguing Old World ambiance. Trimmed with tile, the stone niche contains the shower.

OPPOSITE A pale blue-gray background studded with luminous stars contributes to the serenity and calm of a master bathroom. The silver-toned mirror frame and wall sconce enhance the look.

choosing patterns

After you've settled on a color scheme, you can look for wallpaper and fabrics
to carry through your theme. Two major factors in deciding which patterns to choose
are the location and size of the room. Look at the adjoining areas, especially the ones
that you must pass through to get to the bathroom. Think of them sequentially. If you
want stripes in the bath but the adjoining hallway has a floral wallpaper, match the
colors. In a small bathroom, a bold print may be too busy. On the other hand, it may
be just what is needed to make an extralarge space feel cozy. Vertical designs will add
height to a room. Conversely, horizontal motifs will draw the eye around it. In general,
patterned wallpaper looks best in a traditional-style decor. In a contemporary scheme,
subtle patterns that don't detract from the architecture and the materials are best. And
avoid trendy looks, unless you want to make changes every couple of years.

Choose a window treatment and control system that will both enhance your comfort while in the bathroom and help create the design expression that you are seeking. You can take your first cue from the climate where you live. In a hot climate, window treatments should block heavy direct sunlight, especially if the room faces south or west. In a cool climate, you'll need insulated window treatments to block drafts during the winter, especially if the bathroom faces

window treatments

north. Next consider privacy. If your bath window is visible from the yard or neighboring house, choose a device that can be easily closed to block all views to the interior. Your final selection will have to accommodate the type and size of your windows, the appearance you want, and your budget. Of course, for the bath, it's always best to choose easy-clean materials.

LEFT If privacy isn't an issue, there is no better finishing touch for a country bath than filmy white café curtains hung from a decorative rod.

ABOVE Standard horizontal-slat blinds suit the traditional look of this older bath and can be easily adjusted to suit the time of day.

ABOVE RIGHT In addition to adding charm, wooden shutters with adjustable slats safeguard privacy while admitting light and air.

RIGHT A fabric roll-up shade is a pretty way to provide privacy. This one can be easily removed from the tension rod for cleaning.

window treatments add a finishing touch

OPPOSITE In a bath with traditional style, a tie-back curtain at the window provides a soft touch of elegance and doesn't obstruct the use of the window crank.

FAR LEFT As illustrated by this curtain-and-wallcovering duo, two different patterns can harmonize side by side if they have colors in common.

LEFT Understated pleated shades suit the streamlined look of casement windows and can stand alone on style or pair harmoniously with a fabric treatment.

BELOW LEFT Neat and tailored Roman shades can be raised or lowered easily.

BELOW In an older house, a tall window admits abundant light; solid-panel wood shutters on the lower half close for privacy.

If functionality were the only requisite for a bedroom, nothing would be needed other than a bed, side table, and dresser. In today's multitasking world, however, bedrooms are so much more. Exercising, watching TV, paying bills, relaxing with family, and providing storage are some of the other activities that might be considered when planning a well-intentioned bedroom. That said, it is important to create an environment for a good night's sleep at the top of the list of design priorities. This chapter presents attractive solutions for a room that is conducive to your personal comfort.

Bedrooms

I your sanctuary I a quality sleep I
I kids' rooms I baby rooms I

The calming blue-and-white decorating scheme is key to this relaxing environment. The orderly arrangement of furniture and the lack of clutter add to the room's restful ambiance.

your sanctuary

If not the bedroom, where else can you go to escape the pressures and tribulations of daily life? Few places offer the privacy and quiet of a bedroom, and these are the qualities that make it an ideal personal retreat. Start with a feeling—the sense you get when you are in a calm, restful environment. Try to create this ambiance through your choice of colors, textures, furniture, and accessories.

Color is perhaps the most obvious and easiest place to begin because it will influence other decorating decisions you will have to make for the room. Does a particular color make you feel happy or sad? If so, use it or lose it in your overall color scheme. Maybe you prefer a subdued singular hue for a palette that encourages contemplation and introspection. Or you might want to incorporate two or more colors throughout your decor to unify the space.

If you have a spacious master suite, use furniture to create intimacy within the room. Choose a large four-poster bed with a canopy for an intimate retreat. Group chairs in a corner for cozy conversation or reading. Transform a corner into a dressing room complete with a wardrobe and privacy screen. In smaller rooms, the same rule applies: the more furniture, the smaller the space will appear. If you need room to breathe, keep furnishings spare and simple.

LEFT Wool wall-to-wall carpeting with a trellis-style motif enhances the room's comfort and underscores the English country-inspired decor. The pattern play among all of the textiles in the room is sophisticated and subtle.

ABOVE This master bedroom's cozy sun-filled bay is an excellent spot for a small table and chairs that can be set for breakfast, afternoon tea, or a spot of warm cocoa before bedtime.

RIGHT The bed is clearly the focal point of the room. A scalloped rod-pocket valance and drapery panels hang ceiling-height above the headboard to create drama. The treatment matches the room's curtains.

LEFT This Adirondack-style four poster bed only looks rustic. Actually, great care was taken to provide the ultimate comfort with plush bedding, lots of fabric as in the bed curtains and dust ruffle, and numerous nature-themed accessories.

ABOVE Some sleep experts discourage keeping a TV or a computer in the bedroom, but it's a personal choice.

OPPOSITE For the sense of a true getaway, this room is somewhat unconventional and exotic looking. The platform bed features a plush down-filled bed pillow. An imported folding screen takes the place of a headboard.

10 tips for a pampering getaway

From accessories to color to textures, there are a number of options you can explore when creating a personal sanctuary.

1. **Get the light right.** Harsh overhead light will kill any chance of creating a cozy, restful retreat. Likewise, too little light will make the room dark and drab. Find a balance by inviting natural light in and supplying supplemental lighting at the bedside, on a table in a sitting area, and on a dressing table.

2. **Fine linens** suggest luxury and decadence—two qualities conducive to rest and relaxation.

3. **Keep accessories** to a minimum. Too many distractions can take away from a soothing atmosphere.

4. **Pay attention to texture.** The simple pleasure of touch does much to make a room feel restful.

5. **Surround yourself** with things you love. A favorite color, a photograph that reminds you of a special trip—whatever makes you smile is a good addition to a personal retreat.

6. **Privacy is essential** even if you share the room or use it for family time, it is important to insist on privacy or quiet at certain times. Hang a hotel-style sign on the doorknob, or simply announce what time of day the room is off limits.

7. **Neutral colors** suggest serenity, but if you have an affinity for a certain color, don't be afraid to use it. Indeed, wrapping a room in a color you love can be just as relaxing.

8. **Add furniture** that invites lounging—a chaise or plump chairs with plush cushions and pillows and a throw are ideal for catnaps and kicking back.

9. **Use natural elements** such as plants, wood furniture, and all-cotton linens. Few materials can top the elegance and appeal of Mother Nature.

10. **Direct seating** or your bed toward the window to encourage meditation and provide a peaceful focal point.

a quality sleep

According to the Better Sleep Council (BSC), judge the quality of a mattress by its coil count—generally, the higher the better—along with the quality of the upholstery material. "Layers of material provide the insulation and cushioning between your body and the spring system," says BSC.

A good night's sleep is one of life's simple pleasures. To set the stage for rest and relaxation in your bedroom, start with the most essential element: the mattress. Whether firm or soft, what matters most is how comfortable the mattress feels to you. Before making a purchase, test-drive the mattress by lying down on it, taking pillows with you if needed to simulate positions that you find most restful. Your weight should be supported evenly; when you roll from side to side, you should not be able to feel coils. With regard to size, consider how much room each sleeper requires to be comfortable and whether multiple pillows are needed for peaceful sleep.

After the mattress, linens are key to restful slumber. Ironically, most people choose linens for their looks, and while coordination is important, how linens feel should be a factor when purchasing them. Look for crisp, clean linens that soothe the skin and blankets and comforters that provide warmth without seeming stuffy. Good-quality sheets generally have a thread count of at least 200 threads per inch, and while there are numerous fibers and materials on the market, nothing can top the longevity and luxurious feel of 100 percent cotton. Dress your bed in layers so that you can remove or add coverings as needed to adjust your comfort throughout the night.

One last item that deserves forethought is a pillow. Down, synthetic fibers, and polyfil are the most common types of fill found in pillows, but again, the most important consideration when choosing a pillow is how it feels when you are lying on it. The right pillow should support your head and keep it in natural alignment with your spine. If you feel pressure on your shoulder when lying on your side, your pillow is too thin. Likewise, if your head is cocked at a sharp angle, your pillow is too thick.

RIGHT If you are considering a vintage bed like this one, be prepared to pay for a custom-made mattress and foundation. Today's standard-size mattresses and foundations probaby won't fit an old bed. Check the measurements before buying—or switch to a reproduction style that has the charm but not the hassles of an antique bed.

bright idea

pillow talk

Use lots of attractive throw pillows to dress up the bed. Mix in different colors, sizes, shapes, and patterns for interest. When you're relaxing in bed reading a book or watching TV, use these extra little cushions to prop up your head or support the small of your back. Washable covers are practical, too.

special amenities add more comfort

ABOVE Lovely lavendar silk was used to dress this bed to match the curtains. Using rich or luxurious-materials for the bedding is one way to pamper yourself. But some of these materials are delicate and must be professionally cleaned.

RIGHT Breakfast in bed, even if it's once in a while, will make you feel as if you're on vacation—if for only an hour. Bring in fresh flowers on the weekend to create an at-home getaway.

LEFT A foostool at the end of each bed can provide additional seating, a place for an extra blanket, or a low table for a tray of snacks or a laptop computer.

BOTTOM LEFT If space allows, create a separate sitting area. A roomy chaise longue, an upholstered chair, and a small table provide an additional place to relax or chat. This keeps the bed neat and reserved for sleeping.

BOTTOM RIGHT A small alcove in this bedroom has been outfitted with an upholstered seat and throw pillows. Although it's hardly roomy enough for napping, it's a comfortble extra seat.

give a master bedroom extra flair

OPPOSITE Imported contemporary furniture has a slick laminate finish in this room. The tray ceiling above the bed has lighting that is reflected on the ceiling for dramatic effect. The small recessed fixtures can be dimmed for quiet relaxing or brightened as needed.

ABOVE LEFT AND RIGHT When not in use, a firebox becomes a nook for fresh or dried flowers— a pretty accent and a clever way to fill an unattractive black hole. The room has direct access to a porch.

RIGHT A winding iron staircase leading to a bedroom loft area in a large master suite creates an interesting focal point. Curtains soften the wall behind the iron bed and match the bedskirt.

LEFT Do you have a small spare room? A twin-size bed and a side table may be all you need to make a weekend guest comfortable.

BELOW Bright colors and patterns make a simple space appealing. A jazzy lamp and cheerful flowers supply informal elegance.

OPPOSITE Your weekend house should be simple but comfortable, too. Here, an adjacent deck makes the place all the more relaxing. Window treatments are spare—just shades or blinds that can be rolled up to let in the sunshine.

guest rooms

Give guests a thoughtful place of their own to sleep, work, or just relax alone by accenting a bedroom with graceful touches—an alarm clock, books by the bedside, a set of fluffy towels for bathing. These small details welcome your guests in style.

The luxury of having a guest room in your house gives you the freedom to decorate in a completely different style than in your own bedroom. And it allows you to pamper your guests with a space that caters to them. Start with a quality bed, mattress, pillows, and linens. Give special thought to color and furniture that you find delightful.

Don't forget about function. A desk for working at their laptop, a comfortable chair for lounging, a radio (or a TV), and magazines will make them feel at home. So will closet space, even if it's not an entire closet. Stock a basket with small amenities, too: a toothbrush, shampoos, nice soaps, and fresh towels. Keep clutter to a minimum so that the room feels and looks fresh.

The best part about this room is that if overnight guests are rare, you can use it as your own retreat for an afternoon or a weekend.

kids' rooms

A child's room poses the perfect opportunity for creating a fantasyland. Indeed, whatever your child adores—sports, horses, dolls, or even cartoon characters—can easily become the impetus for your decorating. That, of course, is the secret: taking your decorating cue from your child. He or she will spend the most time in the space, hence the need to make the room cheerful and welcoming.

Equally important is how the room will be used. Homeowners often get caught up in the decorating theme, only to realize afterward that the room doesn't meet their child's needs. In addition to sleeping, a child's bedroom is typically a place for studying, playing games, working on the computer, hanging out with friends, and reading. Make sure your decorating plan addresses these activities up front.

Choosing furniture with longevity in mind will save you time and money. It might be fun to decorate a nursery with a pricey crib and changing table, but those pieces will be outgrown in two years. Make transitional purchases that meet your needs without breaking your budget, then invest in the best furniture for pieces like a desk, headboard, and dresser that will adapt to the child's needs as he or she grows.

The least expensive and easiest way to change the look of a room is with bedding. Find something that coordinates with other pieces in the room or sets the tone for your decorating scheme. Above all, select washable materials.

OPPOSITE The red-white-and-blue theme of this room is complemented by the patriotic flourishes of a flag headboard and star wall hangings.

ABOVE Use details to carry the theme throughout the room. This throw pillow repeats the star motif from the wall hangings above the bed.

bright idea

have fun with it

The element of surprise creates a lasting impact. Arrange furniture in an unexpected way; apply unique paint textures to walls; use wallpaper in out-of-the-ordinary places; and use unconventional window treatments for fun.

playful happy themes create fun rooms

OPPOSITE Reminiscent of a cottage garden, this bedroom is topped with a ceiling covered in floral wallpaper, a trick that defines the theme without overwhelming the small room.

ABOVE LEFT A few well-placed accessories, like the hand-painted cottage atop the dresser, pull the look together.

ABOVE A sheer canopy not only ties the floral wallpaper on the ceiling to the bedspreads but also unifies the two beds flanking each wall in the room.

LEFT Who could guess that the "cottage" houses a television inside? Keeping the look streamlined cuts down on visual distractions in the room.

use strong color to kick up the look

OPPOSITE Deep blue is the dominant color in this room, but to keep it from being too powerful, the walls are painted only half-way up. Red and shades of white temper the blue's intensity.

ABOVE Distressed finishes allow the coordinating colors to peek through while also adding to the look of Americana.

ABOVE RIGHT A headboard made from wooden pickets and painted to resemble the American flag creates an obvious focal point for the room.

RIGHT A red-rimmed chalkboard adds a playful touch and provides a nice contrast to the blue paneled wall.

bright idea
more is better

Don't stop your decorating theme at what you can see—continue it in adjacent spaces. In this nautical-themed room, the closet is also ship-shape, with cubbies for clothing and toys much like those found on an actual ship.

LEFT The sophisticated choice of artwork, bedding, and accessories gives this youngster's room its nautical theme without seeming too juvenile.

TOP RIGHT The painted blue sky above alludes to the skies a sailor might see. The faux finish is achieved with simple sponging.

RIGHT A place for everything and everything in its place—that's the reasoning behind a closet filled with cubbies and drawers. Shelves are ideal for closet storage because they can hold a variety of items, including clothing, plastic bins filled with art supplies, blankets, and shoes.

OPPOSITE A pastel harlequin design painted from floor to ceiling has the effect of drawn curtains—a perfect backdrop for a young girl's royal retreat.

RIGHT A dresser decked with a mossy vignette lends three-dimensional details to the royal theme

BELOW Ornate buttons hot-glued to the wall on top of each heart lend depth and dimension to the harlequin backdrop.

BELOW RIGHT A bunny queen oversees her royal subjects from her post along a wall in the room.

make the room magical

bright idea

an artful hand

Painted finishes transform a room into a wonderland. Think of walls as blank canvases that can convey your theme in the most realistic way through murals and motifs.

baby rooms

What could be sweeter than a baby crib decked out in ruffles and bows? More than any other design project, planning a room to welcome a new baby is an intense emotional experience. That is why it is so easy to go overboard on decorating and the

budget. Knowing this at the start will help you keep both your sentimental feelings and your checkbook in line when you're planning the nursery.

As with an older child's room, themes are an easy way to decorate, especially inasmuch as there are so many options available. If you find bedding and accessories you like, use them as inspiration for color and accessories in the room. Visiting a fabric store is another way to formulate a decorating plan. From Victorian scenes to retro geometrics, fabrics can trigger an idea that can lead to a unique look for your baby. Period rooms are also a consideration. If you have a collection of Danish modern furniture, use it as a springboard for window treatments, rugs, and bedding that reflect the same period style as the rest of the house.

Soft colors are the most popular choice for baby rooms, but in reality, babies can see only stark contrasts in the first months of life. Black and white, red and white, and deep blue and white are appropriate developmental choices. The same is true for motifs. A toile with a pastoral scene is lovely, but strong shapes are easier for a baby to see.

OPPOSITE A soft blue and yellow color palette form the decorating foundation for this nursery. Keeping the colors and patterns simple makes the room design flexible and gender neutral.

LEFT A window bench is a charming addition to the baby's room, especially when it's paired with a matching sconce. For now, it serves as seating for story time, but as your child grows, it can be used as a homework nook where a small desk can replace the seat or bench that is there now.

BELOW Use textiles to create or reinforce the baby room's decorating theme. This adorable hooked rug can be used on the nursery floor or framed as art and hung on the nursery room wall.

design an enchanting nursery

OPPOSITE The elegance of toile is not limited to adult rooms. Here, coordinating fabrics and wallpaper featuring a youthful scene in toile let you create a sophisticated retreat for baby.

ABOVE White furniture, pastel bed linens, and soft details in the wallpaper and border contribute to the light and airy feel of this charming nursery.

RIGHT The bold blue-and-white-striped check on the cotton rug coordinates with the pattern on the crib linens.

how to choose a quality crib

Today's cribs have as many options and add-ons as automobiles, with hefty price tags to match. What's a new parent to do? Here are some guidelines.

Your first concern should be safety. New cribs will feature the latest safety precautions, but if you get a crib second-hand or use an antique, be sure that the slats are less than 2⅜ inches apart so that your baby's head can't fit through them. With regard to any crib you use, latches to drop the side must lock securely in place. The mattress should be firm and fit snugly, with less than an inch between its sides and the sides of the crib. Make sure the finish is smooth, with no peeling paint, jagged edges, and missing or loose screws. Add-ons such as rolling castors, drawers, and detachable canopies are convenient but not essential features.

There are standard cribs, with head- and footboards; convertible cribs that transition to toddler and full-size beds; canopy cribs, with an ethereal canopy cascading from the top; and round and oval cribs valued for their distinctive shapes. The more unique or custom the crib, the more you can expect to pay.

nursery essentials

There are many expenses associated with putting together a nursery, and furniture and accessories account for only one part of the budget. Fortunately, the absolute necessities are few. Start with these basics, and fill in later with those things you discover will make it easier and more comfortable for you to care for your baby.

- Crib
- Changing Table
- Comfortable Chair, Rocker, or Glider
- Chest of Drawers
- Side Table
- General Lighting
- Flooring
- Table Lamp
- Mobile
- Baby Monitor

OPPOSITE TOP A nursery should be a place of comfort and serenity, not only for baby, but also for the parents. After all, this is where you will spend a large amount of time with your new infant, rocking, changing, and cuddling.

OPPOSITE BOTTOM Stuffed animals, leopard print bedding, and a painted backdrop for the crib suggest a jungle theme.

ABOVE Frills and femininity abound in this nursery, where the furniture, walls, and window treatments can be used later in a young girl's room. The green and pink palette is always a feminine favorite.

invest in versatile furniture

Buying furniture that can serve different roles at various times during your child's development is a clever investment for a nursery. Cribs that convert to junior beds and changing tables with drawers that offer storage space are a few options.

OPPOSITE A changing table with trim around the sides and back can later be used as a chest by simply removing the foam pad from the top.

RIGHT Think about using furniture in unconventional ways or settings, such as bringing a metal outdoor chair inside to add a dash of color.

create a nursery sample board

▌ **Use white foam-core** presentation board that's sold in art-supply stores. One that measures 8½ x 11 inches is ideal for the job. Glue swatches of fabric, paint-color chips, and wallpaper samples to it. Designate about two-thirds of the board for the wall and window treatments, and divide the remaining third between the furnishings, including the crib linens, and the flooring, including area rugs.

▌ **Remove and replace** swatches and samples as you experiment with different looks, prints, and colors. Review the sample board at different times of the day, under various light conditions.

▌ **Pick one main paint color,** and get a sample of it in every tone and shade you can find.

▌ **Remember,** professionals get a lot of their ideas through trial and error.

8

Little more than 20 years ago, a home office was almost unheard of. Yet thanks to technology and the ability to do all kinds of work in a telecommuting capacity, today's home is incomplete without one. At the least, a home office may consist of a couple of drawers designated for files and a countertop that can hold a laptop, mail, and books. But it may also be a dedicated room with built-in cabinetry, spacious workspace, and other amenities that make it an efficient and enjoyable place to conduct business. This chapter offers an assortment of ways to accommodate your work needs at home.

Workspaces

❚ the dedicated home office ❚
❚ the kitchen office ❚

A built-in desk in the kitchen is conducive to both work and overseeing family activities. Drawers and shelves keep office supplies and files organized.

You may not have an array of resources at your fingertips as you might find in a conventional office, but a home office has one greater advantage: you get to do things your way. If you adore the color red, no one can stop you from painting every wall and stick of furniture in this energetic color. If you want to spread your papers and files on the floor and leave them there for weeks, so be it. Indeed, stamping your personal style on the space you occupy most is one of the luxuries of working from home.

Rather than simply set up shop in a spare room, begin by going over your unique needs and arranging and decorating your office to accommodate them. If you find that a view of the outdoors prompts your creative side, position your desk in front of a window. If you like to lounge while reading, make room for a comfortable chair. If timelines, bulletins, and calendars help you manage projects more efficiently, hang plenty of bulletin boards or cover your desk in plexiglass or paper so that you can track important dates and information with written notes.

the dedicated home office

When deciding what to add and what to leave out, think about the stages of your work— what motivates you to start a project, the accoutrements you require to do a job successfully, and how you plan to manage the paperwork and files from a job that inevitably are needed for future reference. The answers to these questions will help you determine the furniture and setup for your workspace.

LEFT Extra seating is a must if you see clients in your home or need a place to ruminate away from the work in front of you.

RIGHT This home office has all the elements for an effective workspace: bookshelves, a desk, ample lighting, a comfortable office chair, and a calming decor.

at home in the office

bright idea

thoughtful design

Decorate your office just as you would any room in your home. Look for proper furniture—pieces that are comfortable and attractive. Choose finishes that require little care. This personal touch will create a professional working environment.

OPPOSITE Dark wood-paneled walls and built-in bookcases are complemented by the formal style of the desk and window treatments in this professional home office.

RIGHT In a kitchen, a section of the cabinetry has been designed for handling household paperwork.

work at home

With the number of people who spend all or part of the work week at home steadily on the rise, the availability of products that can help turn any room in your home into an office has burgeoned. Shop in retail stores and specialty catalogs to find storage items that suit the style of your home and your work habits. Good storage will not only help you work more efficiently, it will keep the office from intruding on the serenity of your home and vice versa. Effective home-office organization and specialized storage also prevent wasted time spent looking for (or worse yet, losing) important items or documents. Here are some additional tips to help you plan optimal office storage:

▌ **Arrange** the furnishings so that you can easily reach as much of what you use on a daily basis as possible (phone, files, reference material) without leaving your chair. When you select furniture, keep in mind that an L-shaped desk arrangement is the most functional.

▌ **Store** supplies in labeled boxes, baskets, or bins. Store backup supplies, such as extra paper and printer cartridges, tucked away in a closet.

▌ **Avoid** wasted wall space. Extend shelves from the floor to the ceiling.

▌ **Plan** on more drawers and shelves than you need right now to allow for expansion so that you don't outgrow your home office too quickly.

ABOVE You can build a small desk and shelves to fit between two storage cabinets.

TOP RIGHT A secretary features both workspace for laptop computers and deep drawers for filing.

RIGHT Well-conceived furnishings can house a multitude of home office functions. Shelves, access for electrical cords, and a slide-out tray for a keyboard transform this reproduction antique armoire into a home office. When the doors are closed, the office is out of sight.

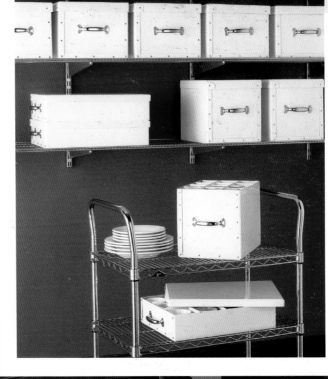

filing facts

Choose filing cabinets based on the value and quantity of what you will be storing.

▌ **Set files up with a system** that makes sense to you. Divide drawers by broad categories, and file by function. One simple organizing tool: color-coded file folders. For a quick and easy point of reference, choose a different color for each category. And label all folders clearly with block-printed letters in a nonsmearing, waterproof ink. File the newest items at the front of the folder, keeping the oldest ones at the back.

▌ **File folders are most efficient** to use if you hang them in a rack that clearly shows off the label. Files that are stacked quickly become a jumble.

▌ **Weed dead files out** of the active filing system and then out of your office as promptly as possible. Transfer them into cardboard banker's boxes; label and date them; and send them to the great filing cabinet in the sky (the attic, of course). Once a year, review these archives and throw out the boxes that hold papers that no longer have a use.

TOP RIGHT Metal shelving, an inexpensive option for storage, has a modern appeal that is enhanced with the orderly placement of bins and boxes to hide clutter.
▌
RIGHT Intense orange on the wall adds a pop of energetic color behind the standard-issue filing cabinets and adjustable shelving.

build a basic bookcase

The case shown here is made with ¾-inch plywood, with a ½-inch plywood back panel and a face-frame made of one-by hardwood boards. The shelves are attached with screws driven through the side pieces. Wood plugs hide the screw heads. If you want to install multiple units, add plugs to only the exposed sides of the end units.

❚ **Assembly.** To build the bookcase, cut the side pieces ½ inch wider than the shelf depth to create a recess for the back panel. Cut the shelves and top piece to size. (Shelves over 32 inches wide will require mid-supports.) If desired, add nosing trim or veneer tape to hide the front edges of the shelves. Assemble the carcase with coarse-thread drywall screws driven through counterbored pilot holes. Cut the back panel; make sure the carcase is square; then attach the panel with glue and brads. Also nail through the back panel into the shelves. You can install 1x2 mounting cleats underneath the bottom shelf and above the top shelf for more strength.

❚ **Installation.** Install the case by screwing through the mounting cleats and into the wall framing. Install the face-frame with glue and finishing nails. You can preassemble the frame using biscuits or install it one piece at a time. Add molding or one-by trim boards along the top and, if desired, along the bottom of the case. Match any existing base molding to create a built-in look.

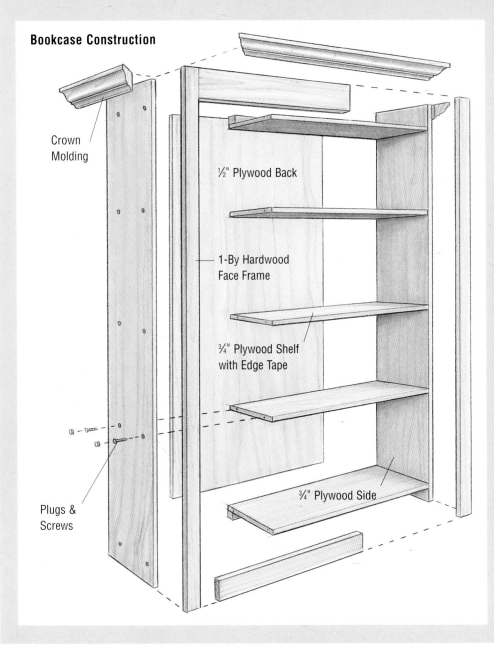

Bookcase Construction

Crown Molding

½" Plywood Back

1-By Hardwood Face Frame

¾" Plywood Shelf with Edge Tape

¾" Plywood Side

Plugs & Screws

OPPOSITE Open bookshelves are convenient because they place books at your fingertips, and they transform the books themselves into decorating accessories. Make sure the shelves are sturdy enough to withstand the weight of books.

bright idea

let there be light

For interest, layer a room with light. When you include multiple light sources in your decorating plan, your office will look, feel, and function better. But avoid light sources that produce glare on your work surface.

▌▌ diverse light sources create ambiance ▌▐▐▐▐▐▐▐▐▐▐▐▐▐▐▐▐▐▐▐▐

take two

There are two common types of lighting to consider for your office. *Indirect light,* also called diffused or ambient light, illuminates the room without focusing on a specific place or task. *Direct light*, or task or accent lighting, highlights a certain object or area in the room. Use both to eliminate shadows and to create appropriate light sources for both day and nighttime activity.

OPPOSITE TOP A wall cabinet becomes a focal point when the accent lighting glows. A table lamp provides task lighting.
▌
OPPOSITE BOTTOM Two lamps have a practical purpose—directing light onto the desktop—but their distinct design makes them decorative as well.
▌
LEFT By day, natural light floods the room through an unadorned window. By night, accent lighting plays up the painted mural on the vaulted ceiling.

the care of books

Here are some guidelines for keeping your library—whether it's an entire room lined with built-in bookcases or a single shelf unit next to a cozy chair—in good shape. Remember: books are sensitive to environmental factors.

❙ **Because humidity** and extreme temperatures are books' enemies, try not to position bookcases against an outside wall, which is often prone to temperature fluctuations.

❙ **Shield books** from strong light (natural or artificial) to keep the bindings from fading.

❙ **To prevent warping,** stand books of like sizes together on a shelf packed neither too tightly nor too loosely.

❙ **Don't push books** all the way to the back of shelves where ventilation might be minimal; over time, mold could form.

❙ **Store fragile** or large and heavy volumes flat.

❙ **For an elegant touch,** display a particularly significant or attractive book on a stand.

LEFT A plethora of bookcases suggest the need for a comfortable place to read, hence the overstuffed loveseat in the office.
❙
OPPOSITE Recessed bookcases flanking the walls of this office act much the same as wallpaper, adding to the style and verve of the room. Low-voltage strip lighting highlights them. The floor-to-ceiling height of the display also draws the eye upward to the painted ceiling—a handsome custom touch.

the kitchen office

I n many homes, the kitchen is family central, a place where children do their homework and you sort through the mail and even pay the bills. These multiple uses are all the more reason to integrate an office nook within the kitchen. If you are designing a kitchen layout from scratch, position your office space near a door for convenient dropping of mail and out of the way of other kitchen functions. If you are repurposing space in your existing kitchen, identify a portion of a countertop that gets less use than other spaces and designate it as your office. If possible, snag shelf space or a section of the cabinetry for a computer, supplies, and even file drawers.

OPPOSITE TOP A desk has been built onto the end of this large island. It's a great spot for planning menus, answering mail, and keeping track of household expenses.

OPPOSITE BOTTOM When this kitchen was remodeled, the homeowner requested a small built-in desk, which is located at the end of a run of cabinetry.

BELOW A small countertop with space underneath and a corkboard backsplash is an efficient use of kitchen space. The cabinets and cubbies above it can hold files, the mail, and recipe books.

Good design doesn't end at the door. Indeed, decorators include decks, porches, sunrooms, and patios as part of a home's layout and often incorporate them into the overall design scheme. Not only do these outdoor rooms deserve the same design attention as interior spaces, they require additional thought because much of their ambiance is dependant on the climate. But with careful planning, your home's outdoor rooms have the potential to become your favorite living spaces. Here are some stylish ideas for decks, patios, and other open-air spaces.

Outdoor Style

▌ dressing up the outdoors ▌
▌ porches and sunrooms ▌

A comfortable chair on the front porch provides an excellent place to relax. Plump cushions and pillows covered in a treated all-weather fabric enhance the comfort.

apply all of the elements of good design

Making elements from a few different architectural styles work cohesively can be done successfully if you follow the basic principals of good design, whether you're updating the interior or exterior spaces of your home.

Start with *scale* and *proportion*. These two principals work together. Scale refers to size. Proportion refers to the relationship of parts or elements based on size. For example, if you're planning to build a covered entry or porch, make sure it's the right size for the existing house. You can apply this principal to landscaping and hardscaping projects as well as to outdoor ornamentation.

Line is another important design element. Add sophistication to your home by incorporating linear interest. Create vertical lines using tall columns, conical trees, or shutters; emphasize horizontal lines by adding a strong balustrade or a platform in front of an entrance; suggest diagonal lines with with a gabled roofline; and make curved lines using a scalloped flower bed or curved walkway.

Use your own judgment and good eye to maintain *balance* and *harmony*.

LEFT A gambrel roof on each end of this Dutch Colonial home gives it a symmetrical appearance.

ABOVE LEFT An elliptical window balances the off-center entry.

TOP A red door welcomes visitors to this home.

ABOVE A cylindrical light adds interest.

BELOW The window's oval shape complements the formal facade.

ABOVE LEFT An antique door, such as this oak beauty, was restored to its original warm honey grain to make a fitting entrance to this grand old house.

ABOVE RIGHT An original stained-glass window was trimmed in a warm cream. It gains grandeur from gold-leaf accenting.

BELOW The floors and handrails, stripped and stained in hues that complement the age and stature of the house, bring added warmth to the large porch.

ABOVE An old house, rich in architectural detail, wears a meticulous application of new paint and color like a crown. Some of the surfaces, such as the porch floor and ceiling, the stairs, and the porch rail cap, were stained a deep chestnut color to add richness to the wood.

old paint

There are several ways to strip layers of old paint. Chemicals soften the paint so that you can scrape it. A heat gun does the same thing without chemicals. Then there's sandpaper, sharp scrapers, power washers, and more. The trick is to pick the most practical method for your job. On large surfaces, such as the side of a house, applying gallons of caustic chemicals would make a mess and be difficult to handle. Those surfaces should be power washed or scraped. Chemical strippers and heat are better for small jobs, such as removing layers of paint from molding. Where grooves and other details in the wood are almost filled with old paint, you may need several applications. On flat surfaces, you can use a putty knife to clear the softened paint. In tight spots, use a shaped scraper blade. There are hand-held models and tools with interchangeable heads designed to dig into all kinds of beading and channels. Before stripping, be sure that the paint is not lead-based. Have a sample checked if you're uncertain. Also bear in mind that your town may have restrictions on disposing of the waste. If you use a chemical stripper, always wear rubber gloves and a safety mask.

dressing up the outdoors

For a dynamic change in the look of your house, no element packs more punch than color, and few design tools are as satisfying to exploit. You can use color in ways that are either subtle or strong. But one thing is for sure: color is always personal. And while there are some guidelines to keep you on track in terms of combining colors and complementing certain architectural styles, the field is usually wide open to your preferences. (Be careful: some localities, especially historic areas, mandate what colors you can paint your house.) Start exploring your options here.

ABOVE On a large front porch, there are two furniture groupings to create intimate circles for conversation. Each area has its own seating pieces and a table for resting snacks.

RIGHT Wicker is classic on a front porch. A wide-striped cotton duck fabric on the chair cushions has a traditional summer look. Red toss pillows perk up the neutral scheme.

OPPOSITE A wraparound porch on a turn-of-the-century cottage is charming. The bead-board ceiling has been painted baby blue—an old-fashioned tradition meant to mimic the color of the sky.

porch style

Shade is perhaps a porch's number one purpose, but eating and visiting are close seconds. Follow these tips to decorate your porch so that it is conducive to these activities and many more.

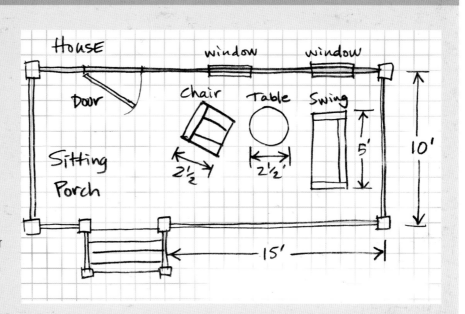

- **Forgo the fold-up metal chairs** and rickety side tables for a mix of furniture that makes the space feel like a room.
- **Use an outdoor rug** to anchor the seating area and delineate space.
- **Use a table** large enough for dining, and have plenty of chairs on hand for extra guests.
- **Have a buffet** or console handy for mixing drinks and serving lunch buffet-style.
- **Cushion all seats,** and provide floor cushions for lounging.
- **Decorate the porch** with plants to integrate the surrounding landscape.

- **Stock an outdoor armoire** or dresser with games and puzzles for afternoon fun.
- **Paint or stain the floor,** rails, columns, and other exterior trim for a crisp, clean appearance.
- **Keep a basket of books** and magazines on hand for impromptu reading.

bright idea

simply slipcovers

Slipcovers for cushions and pillows that can be removed for laundering are the most practical choice for outdoor seating pieces. Because they are for casual use, their design is simple and not too difficult to sew yourself.

dress up an old door

Does your old front door need TLC? That means a new paint job for starters. If the door has been painted many times, take it off its hinges and strip it before adding more layers of paint. You will have to strip it if you intend to display the original wood. If you can get away with just painting the door, sand it down first and use an exterior latex paint. Once you've got the door itself spruced up, you can fit it with new dorknob and lock hardware, a knocker, or even new glass. Another way to restore a door is to replace the casing— the trim that conceals the gap between the doorjambs and the walls. You can opt for a built-up crosshead—a heavier, detailed horizontal molding that goes over the door and pilasters (right)— and simulated pillars that run along the sides of the door. Some molding manufacturers offer pieces that eliminate the need for any difficult miter cuts.

OPPOSITE These two door knockers share a satin nickel finish but could not be more different from each other. The streamlined look of the far left one is distinctly contemporary, while the ornate example near left takes its cue from older European style.

RIGHT Even a practical item such as a doormat can show off your style. Personalize it with a monogram or your family's name. Choose a design that's in keeping with your decorating style or that says something about you, such as a topiary motif if you like to garden.

BELOW House numbers can really jazz up the front of your house, and they come in numerous styles, sizes, and finishes, such as Arts and Crafts or Colonial. If you want something utterly unique, paint them yourself, as illustrated below.

Porches and sunrooms offer the best of both worlds: the natural light and beauty of nature along with the convenience and comfort of indoors. It is easy to think of these rooms as distinct from interior spaces, but in reality, they should be part of your overall design scheme, especially if they are located adjacent to an interior room or passed through to reach an indoor space. These issues affect their look, furniture arrangement, traffic pattern, and the selection of materials used in the room.

The best way to coax family and friends outside is to create a casual, enjoyable room. Select furniture not only for its attractiveness and durability but also for its comfort. Top wooden and metal chairs and gliders with plump cushions. Coat wicker with paint that both protects and polishes the look. Have ample seating and table space to hold drinks, snacks, and magazines. Hammocks, chaise longues, and even daybeds are other ideas that take advantage of a porch or sunroom's easy, breezy feel. Don't forget lighting, especially if you like to linger outdoors after sunset. Check out the outdoor lamps on the market.

One last consideration is privacy. If this room is located on the front of your home, add curtains that diffuse the light or blinds that can be pulled down when desired. Plant a privacy hedge that hides the room from the street, or fashion screens from salvaged shutters for a cottage-style touch.

porches and sunrooms

OPPOSITE This custom-built conservatory's rich warm tones make this an inviting indoor-outdoor living space.

ABOVE LEFT Outdoor fireplaces are hotter than ever. This stone fireplace also doubles as a traditional pizza oven.

ABOVE RIGHT Windows and skylights take the place of conventional walls and ceilings in this all-purpose sunroom. Because the room is closed off to the elements, indoor furniture and light fixtures can be used in the decor, but adjustable shades may be necessary to prevent them from fading.

RIGHT A limestone tile floor is cool under foot and lemon-color walls are cheerful inside this covered veranda. Casual furnishings look like they could be equally at home indoors.

RIGHT Curves add distinction to trellis and arbor designs. Some manufacturers match curves or other elements from their arbors with elements on fences. This design is the perfect way to create an entry into a garden room.

BELOW LEFT Simple designs combined with high-quality materials and workmanship lead to attractive and functional garden structures. You can combine them in different configurations to delineate separate outdoor living spaces.

BELOW RIGHT Metal trellises allow for unique designs, such as this sun motif.

ABOVE A deck seating area can be dressed up with cushions. This design gets a lift from a custom pergola roof.

ABOVE RIGHT Add unusual shapes or ornament to garden beds to create interest. Metal allows for designs that just aren't possible when working with wood.

RIGHT This pretty arched trellis tower adds a decorative accent outdoors and would look great with or without climbing plants.

Resource Guide

MANUFACTURERS

Above View
414-744-7118
www.aboveview.com
Makes ornamental ceiling tiles.

Adagio, Inc.
www.adagiosinks.com
877-988-2297
Makes hand-crafted sinks in a variety of materials.

All Multimedia Storage
866-603-1700
www.allmultimediastorage.com
Manufactures media storage.

Amana
800-843-0304
www.amana.com
Manufactures refrigerators, dishwashers, and cooking appliances.

American Standard
www.americanstandard-us.com
Manufactures plumbing and tile products.

Amtico International Inc.
404-267-1900
www.amtico.com
Manufactures vinyl flooring.

Ann Sacks Tile & Stone, a division of Kohler
800-278-8453
www.annsacks.com
Manufactures ceramic, glass, and stone tile.

Architectural Products by Outwater
800-835-4400
www.outwater.com
Manufactures hardwood and plastic moldings, niches, frames, hardware, and other architectural products.

Armstrong World Industries
717-397-0611
www.armstrong.com
Manufactures floors, cabinets, ceilings, and ceramic tiles.

Artemide
631-694 9292
www.artemide.com
Manufactures lighting fixtures.

Atlas Homewares
818-240-3500
www.atlashomewares.com
Manufactures house numbers, door knockers, and doorbells.

Bach Faucets
866-863-6584
www.bachfaucet.com
Manufactures faucets.

Ballard Designs
800-536-7551
www.ballarddesigns.com
An online and catalog source for decorative accessories, including boxes and baskets.

Baltic Leisure
800-441-7147
www.balticleisure.com
Manufactures steam showers and saunas.

Bassett Furniture Industries
276-629-6000
www.bassettfurniture.com
Manufactures both upholstered furniture and casegoods.

The following list of manufacturers and associations is meant to be a general guide to additional industry and product-related sources. It is not intended as a listing of products and manufacturers represented by the photographs in this book.

Bemis Manufacturing Co.

800-558-7651

www.bemismfg.com

Manufactures toilet seats.

Benjamin Moore & Co.

www.benjaminmoore.com

Manufactures paint.

Blue Mountain Wallcoverings, Inc.

866-563-9872

www.imp-wall.com

Manufactures wallcoverings under the brand names Imperial, Sunworthy, Katzenbach & Warren, and Sanitas.

Brewster Wallcovering Co.

781-963-4800

www.brewsterwallcovering.com

Manufactures wallpaper, fabrics, and borders in many patterns and styles.

Calico Corners

800-213-6366

www.calicocorners.com

A national retailer specializing in fabric. In-store services include design consultation and custom window-treatment fabrication.

Central Fireplace

800-248-4681

www.centralfireplace.com

Manufactures freestanding and zero-clearance fireplaces.

CoCaLo, Inc.

714-434-7200

Manufactures juvenile bedding under the brand names CoCaLo, Oshkosh B' Gosh, Baby Martex, and Kimberly Grant.

Colebrook Conservatories

800-356-2749

www.colebrookconservatories.com

Designs, builds, and installs fine conservatories, glass enclosures, period glass structures, roof lanterns, and horticultural greenhouses.

Comfortex Window Fashions

800-843-4151

www.comfortex.com

Manufactures custom window treatments, including sheer and pleated shades, wood shutters, and blinds. Its Web site provides company information and a store locator.

Congoleum Corp.

800-274-3266

www.congoleum.com

Manufactures resilient, high-pressure plastic-laminate flooring.

Corian, a division of DuPont

800-426-7426

www.corian.com

Manufactures solid surfacing.

Country Curtains

800-456-0321

www.countrycurtains.com

A national retailer and on-line source for ready-made curtains, draperies, shades, blinds, hardware, and accessories.

Crossville, Inc.

931-484-2110

www.crossvilleinc.com

Manufactures porcelain, stone, and metal tile.

Couristan, Inc.

800-223-6186

www.couristan.com

Manufactures natural and synthetic carpets and rugs.

Dex Studios

404-753-0600

www.dexstudios.com

Creates custom concrete sinks, tubs, and countertops.

Resource Guide

EGS Electrical Group
Easy Heat
860-653-1600
www.easyheat.com
Manufactures floor-warming systems.

Elfa
www.elfa.com
Manufactures storage products.

Elkay
630-574-8484
www.elkayusa.com
Manufactures sinks, faucets, and countertops.

Elyria Fence Inc.
800-779-7581
www.elyriafence.com
Provides custom fences, trellises, arbors, and decks year-round. Its Web site has a photo gallery of its many styles and designs.

Ethan Allen Furniture
888-324-3571
www.ethanallen.com
Manufactures upholstered furniture and casegoods.

Expanko, Inc.
800-345-6202
www.expanko.com
Manufactures cork and rubber flooring.

Finn + Hattie, a division of Maine Cottage
207-846-9166
www.finnandhattie.com
Manufactures juvenile furniture.

Finnleo
800-346-6536

www.finnleo.com
Manufactures saunas, steam baths, and accessories.

Fisher & Paykel, Inc.
888-936-7872
www.fisherpaykel.com
Manufactures kitchen appliances.

Florida Tile
800-242-9042
www.floridatile.com
Distributor and manufacturer of ceramic wall and floor tile.

Formica Corporation
513-786-3525
www.formica.com
Manufactures plastic laminate and solid surfacing.

Garden Artisans
410-721-6185
Fax: 410-451-9535
www.gardenartisans.com
Sells decorative backyard structures such as garden art, trellises, arbors, and planters, including a selection of copper and metal structures.

Gautier
954-975-3303
www.gautierusa.com
Manufactures furniture.

General Electric
580-634-0151
www.ge.com
Manufactures appliances and electronics.

G.I. Designs
877-442-6773
www.gidesigns.net

Manufacturers of wooden and metal garden structures such as trellises, arbors, and gazebos.

Ginger

www.gingerco.com
Manufactures lighting and bathroom accessories.

Glidden

800-454-3336
www.glidden.com
Manufactures paint.

Globus Cork

718-742-7264
www.corkfloor.com
Manufactures cork flooring.

Green Mountain Soapstone Corp.

802-468-5636
www.greenmountainsoapstone.com
Manufactures soapstone floors, walls, sinks, and countertops.

Haier America

877-337-3639
www.haieramerica.com
Manufactures electronics and appliances, including wine cellars.

Häfele America Co.

1-800-423-3531
www.hafeleonline.com
Manufactures cabinet hardware.

Hartco Hardwood Floors

800-769-8528
www.hartcoflooring.com
Manufactures engineered hardwood and solid wood flooring.

Herbeau Creations of America

239-417-5368

www.herbeau.com
Makes vitreous china fixtures.

Hoesch Design

www.hoesch.de
Manufactures tubs and shower partitions.

Hunter Douglas, Inc.

800-789-0331
www.hunterdouglas.com
Manufactures shades, blinds, and shutters. Its Web site directs you to designers, dealers, and installers.

Ikea

www.ikea.com
Manufactures furniture and home-organization accessories.

Jacuzzi Inc.

800-288-4002
www.jacuzzi.com
Manufactures spas and shower systems.

Jenn-Air, a division of Maytag Corp.

Maytag Customer Service
800-688-1100
www.jennair.com
Manufactures kitchen appliances.

Jian & Ling Bamboo

757-368-2060
www.jianlingbamboo.com
Manufactures vertical and horizontal cut bamboo flooring.

Kemiko Concrete Products

903-587-3708
www.kemiko.com
Manufactures acid stains for concrete flooring and other concrete products. Creates decorative concrete floors.

Resource Guide

KidKraft
800-933-0771
www.kidkraft.com
Manufactures children's furniture.

Kirsch Window Fashions
800-538-6567
www.kirsch.com
Manufactures blinds, rods, shades, and holdbacks.

Kohler
800-456-4537
www.kohler.com
Manufactures plumbing products.

Kraftmaid Cabinetry
440-632-5333
www.kraftmaid.com
Manufactures cabinetry.

Lambs and Ivy
800-345-2627
www.lambsandivy.com
Manufactures juvenile bedding, rugs, lamps, and accessories.

Lane Home Furnishings
www.lanefurniture.com
Manufactures both upholstered furniture and casegoods.

Laticrete International, Inc.
203-393-0010
800-243-4788
www.laticrete.com
Manufactures epoxy grout in many colors.

La-Z-Boy
www.la-z-boy.com
Manufactures furniture.

LG
800-243-0000
www.lge.com
Manufactures major appliances.

Lightology
866-954-4489
www.lightology.com
Manufactures lighting fixtures.

Maytag Corp.
800-688-9900
www.maytag.com
Manufactures major appliances.

Merillat
www.merillat.com
Manufactures cabinets.

MGS Progetti
www.mgsprogetti.com
Manufactures stainless-steel faucets.

Moen
800-289-6636
www.moen.com
Manufactures plumbing products.

Motif Designs
800-431-2424
www.motif-designs.com
Manufactures furniture, fabrics, and wallcoverings.

Neo-Metro, a div. of Acorn Engineering Co.
800-591-9050
www.neo-metro.com
Manufactures countertops, tubs, lavs, and tile.

Nuheat Industries, Ltd.
800-778-WARM

www.nuheat.com

Manufactures radiant electric floor heating systems.

NuTone, Inc.
888-336-3948

www.nutone.com

Manufactures ventilation fans, medicine cabinets, and lighting fixtures.

Osram-Sylvania
978-777-1900

www.sylvania.com

Manufactures lighting products and accessories.

PatchKraft
800-866-2229

www.patchkraft.com

Manufactures coordinated bedding for cribs and twin- and full-size beds, using infant-safe fabrics.

Plaid Industries
800-842-4197

www.plaidonline.com

Manufactures stencils, stamps, and craft paints.

Plain and Fancy Custom Cabinetry
800-447-9006

www.plainfancycabinetry.com

Makes custom cabinetry.

Precor USA
800-786-8404

www.precor.com

Manufactures cardiovascular fitness equipment, such as elliptical trainers, for residential and commercial use.

Price Pfister, Inc.
800-732-8238

www.pricepfister.com

Manufactures faucets.

Remcraft Lighting Products
www.remcraft.com

Manufactures lighting fixtures.

Restoration Hardware
800-910-9836

www.restorationhardware.com

Manufactures indoor and outdoor furniture, windows, and lighting accessories.

Robern, a div. of Kohler
www.robern.com

Manufactures medicine cabinets.

Schonbek Worldwide Lighting Inc.
800-836-1892

www.schonbek.com

Manufactures crystal lighting fixtures.

Seabrook Wallcoverings, Inc.
800-238-9152

www.seabrookwallpaper.com

Manufactures borders and wallcoverings.

Seagull Lighting Products, Inc.
856-764-0500

www.seagulllighting.com

Manufactures lighting fixtures.

Sharp
www.sharpusa.com

Manufactures consumer electronics.

Resource Guide

Sherwin-Williams

www.sherwinwilliams.com

Manufactures paint.

Spiegel

Spiegel Customer Satisfaction

800-474-5555

www.spiegel.com

An on-line and paper catalog source of all types of window treatments, hardware, and related embellishments.

Springs Industries, Inc.

888-926-7888

www.springs.com

Manufactures window treatments, including blinds and shutters, and distributes Graber Hardware.

Sonoma Cast Stone

888-807-4234

www.sonomastone.com

Designs and builds concrete sinks and countertops.

Stanley Furniture

276-627-2100

www.stanley.com

Manufactures entertainment centers and other home furniture.

Stencil Ease

800-334-1776

www.stencilease.com

Manufactures laser-cut stencils and related tools and supplies.

Stickley Furniture

315-682-5500

www.stickley.com

Manufactures furniture.

Sub-Zero Freezer Co.

800-222-7820

www.subzero.com

Manufactures professional-style refrigeration appliances.

Sure-Fit, Inc.

888-754-7166

www.surefit.com

Manufactures ready-made slipcovers and pillows.

Tarkett

www.tarkett-floors.com

Manufactures vinyl, laminate, tile, and wood flooring.

Thibaut Inc.

800-223-0704

www.thibautdesign.com

Manufactures wallpaper and fabrics.

Thomasville Furniture Industries

800-225-0265

www.thomasville.com

Manufactures wood and upholstered furniture and casegoods.

Toto USA

770-282-8686

www.totousa.com

Manufactures toilets, bidets, sinks, and bathtubs.

Trellis Structures, Inc.

888-285-4624

www.trellisstructures.com

Designs and manufactures western red cedar trellises and arbors, as well as other structures.

Velux-America

800-888-3589

www.velux.com

Manufactures skylights and solar tunnels.

Viking Range Corp.

www.vikingrange.com

Manufactures professional-style kitchen appliances.

Villeroy and Boch

877-505-5350

www.villeroy-boch.com

Manufactures fixtures, fittings, and furniture.

WarmaTowel, a division of Sussman

800-667-8372

www.nortesco.com/sussman/towel/towel.html

Manufactures towel-warming metal racks.

Warmly Yours

800-875-5285

www.warmlyyours.com

Manufactures radiant floor heating systems.

Watermark Designs, Ltd.

800-842-7277

www.watermark-designs.com

Manufactures faucets and lighting fixtures.

Waterworks

800-998-2284

www.waterworks.com

Manufactures plumbing products.

Waverly Baby

800-423-5881

www.waverly.com

Manufactures bedding, wallcoverings, and window treatments for the nursery.

Whirlpool Corp.

www.whirlpool.com

Manufactures home appliances and related products, including a drying cabinet and an ironing center.

Wilsonart International

800-433-3222

www.wilsonart.com

Manufactures plastic laminate countertops.

Wolf Appliance Company

www.wolfappliance.com

Manufactures professional-style cooking appliances.

Wood-Mode Fine Custom Cabinetry

877-635-7500

www.wood-mode.com

Manufactures custom cabinetry for the kitchen.

York Wallcoverings

717-846-4456

www.yorkwall.com

Manufactures borders and wallcoverings.

ASSOCIATIONS

National Association of Remodeling Industry (NARI)

800-611-6274

www.nari.org

A professional organization for remodelers, contractors, and design-build professionals.

National Kitchen and Bath Association (NKBA)

800-652-2776

www.nkba.org

A national trade organization for kitchen and bath design professionals. It offers consumers product information and a referral service.

Glossary

Accent Lighting: A type of lighting that highlights an area or object to emphasize that aspect of a room's character.

Accessible Designs: Those that accommodate persons with physical disabilities.

Adaptable Designs: Those that can be easily changed to accommodate a person with disabilities.

Analogous Scheme: See Harmonious Color Scheme.

Ambient Lighting: General illumination that surrounds a room. There is no visible source of the light.

Art Deco: A decorative style that was based on geometric forms. It was popular during the 1920s and 1930s.

Art Nouveau: A late-nineteenth-century decorative style that was based on natural forms. It was the first style to reject historical references and create its own design vocabulary, which included stylized curved details.

Arts and Crafts Movement: A decorative style that began in England during the late nineteenth century, where it was known as the Aesthetic Movement. Lead by William Morris, the movement rejected industrialization and encouraged fine craftsmanship and simplicity in design.

Backlighting: Illumination coming from a source behind or at the side of an object.

Backsplash: The vertical part at the rear and sides of a countertop that protects the adjacent wall.

Box Pleat: A double pleat, underneath which the edges fold toward each other.

Broadloom: A wide loom for weaving carpeting that is 54 inches wide or more.

Built-In: Any element, such as a bookcase or cabinetry, that is built into a wall or an existing frame.

Cabriole: A double-curve or reverse S-shaped furniture leg that leads down to an elaborate foot (usually a ball-and-claw type).

Candlepower: The luminous intensity of a beam of light (total luminous flux) in a particular direction, measured in units called candelas.

Casegoods: A piece of furniture used for storage, including cabinets, dressers, and desks.

Clearance: The amount of space between two fixtures, the centerlines of two fixtures, or a fixture and an obstacle, such as a wall.

Code: A locally or nationally enforced mandate regarding structural design, materials, plumbing, or electrical systems that state what you can or cannot do when you build or remodel.

Colonial Style: An early-American architectural and decorative style during the Colonial period that was influenced by design ideas brought by settlers from Europe, particularly England.

Color Wheel: A pie-shaped diagram showing the range and relationships of pigment and dye colors.

Complementary Colors: Hues directly opposite each other on the color wheel. As the strongest contrasts, complements tend to intensify each other.

Contemporary: Any modern design (after 1920) that does not contain traditional elements.

Cove: 1. A built-in recess in a wall or ceiling that conceals an indirect light source. 2. A concave recessed molding that is usually found where the wall meets the ceiling or floor.

Daybed: A bed made up to appear as a sofa. It usually has a frame that consists of a headboard, a footboard, and a sideboard along the back.

Dimmer Switch: A switch that can vary the intensity of the light it controls.

Distressed Finish: A decorative paint technique in which the final paint coat is sanded and battered to produce an aged appearance.

Dovetail: A joinery method in which wedge-shaped parts are interlocked to form a tight bond. This joint is commonly used in furniture making.

Dowel: A short cylinder, made of wood, metal, or plastic, that fits into corresponding holes bored in two pieces of wood, creating a joint.

Faux Finish: A decorative paint technique that imitates a pattern found in nature.

Federal: An architectural and decorative style popular in America during the early nineteenth century, fea-

turing delicate ornamentation and symmetrically arranged rooms.

Fittings: The plumbing devices that bring water to the fixtures, such as faucets.

Fluorescent Lighting: A glass tube coated on the interior with phosphor, a chemical compound that emits light when activated by ultraviolet energy. Air in the tube is replaced with a combination of argon gas and a small amount of mercury.

Focal Point: The dominant element in a room or design, usually the first to catch your eye.

Footcandle: A unit that is used to measure brightness. A footcandle is equal to one lumen per square foot of surface.

Framed Cabinet: A cabinet with a full frame across the face of the cabinet box.

Frameless Cabinet: A cabinet without a face frame. It may also be called a "European-style" cabinet.

Frieze: A horizontal band at the top of the wall or just below the cornice.

Full-Spectrum Light: Light that contains the full range of wavelengths that can be found in daylight, including invisible radiation at the end of each visible spectrum.

Gateleg Table: A drop-leaf table supported by a gate-like leg that folds or swings out.

Georgian: An architectural and decorative style popular in America during the late eighteenth century, with rooms characterized by the use of paneling and other woodwork, and bold colors.

Gothic Revival: An architectural and decorative style popular during the mid-nineteenth century. It romanticized the design vocabulary of the medieval period, using elements such as pointed arches and trefoils (three-leaf motifs).

Greek Revival: An architectural and decorative style that drew inspiration from ancient Greek designs. It is characterized by the use of pediments and columns.

Ground-Fault Circuit Interrupter (GFCI): A safety circuit breaker that compares the amount of current entering a receptacle with the amount leaving. If there is a discrepancy of 0.005 volt, the GFCI breaks the circuit in a fraction of a second. GFCIs are required in damp areas of the house.

Grout: A mortar that is used to fill the spaces between tiles.

Hardware: Wood, plastic, or metal plated trim found on the exterior of furniture, such as knobs, handles, and decorative trim.

Harmonious Color Scheme: Also called analogous, a combination focused on neighboring hues on the color wheel. The shared underlying color generally gives such schemes a coherent flow.

Hue: Another term for specific points on the pure, clear range of the color wheel.

Incandescent Lighting: A bulb (lamp) that converts electric power into light by passing electric current through a filament of tungsten wire.

Indirect Lighting: A more subdued type of lighting that is not head-on, but rather reflected against another surface such as a ceiling.

Inlay: A decoration, usually consisting of stained wood, metal, or mother-of-pearl, that is set into the surface of an object in a pattern and finished flush.

International Style: A post–World War II architectural and decorative style that emphasized simplicity and lacked ornamentation. Smooth surfaces, an extensive use of windows, and white walls are hallmarks of this pared-down style.

Lambrequin: Drapery that hangs from a shelf, such as a mantel, or covering the top of a window or a door. This term is sometimes used interchangeably with valance.

Love Seat: A sofa-like piece of furniture that consists of seating for two.

Lumen: The measurement of a source's light output—the quantity of visible light.

Lumens Per Watt (LPW): The ratio of the amount of light provided to the energy (watts) used to produce the light.

Modular: Units of a standard size, such as pieces of a sofa, that can be fitted together.

Molding: An architectural band used to trim a line where materials join or create a linear decoration. It is typically made of wood, plaster, or a polymer.

Mortise-and-Tenon Joinery: A hole (mortise) cut into a piece of wood that receives a projecting piece (tenon) to create a joint.

Neoclassic: Any revival of the ancient styles of Greece and Rome, particularly during the late eighteenth and early nineteenth centuries.

Occasional Piece: A small piece of furniture for incidental use, such as end tables.

Orientation: The placement of any object or space, such as a window, a door, or a room, and its relationship to the points on a compass.

Panel: A flat, rectangular piece of material that forms part of a wall, door, or cabinet. Typically made of wood, it is usually framed by a border and either raised or recessed.

Parquet: Inlaid woodwork arranged to form a geometric pattern. It consists of small blocks of wood, which are often stained in contrasting colors.

Pattern Matching: To align a repeating pattern when joining together two pieces of fabric.

Pediment: A triangular piece found over doors, windows, and occasionally mantles. It also refers to a low-pitched gable on the front of a building.

Peninsula: A countertop, with or without a base cabinet, that is connected at one end to a wall or another counter and extends outward, providing access on three sides.

Post-Modernism: A term used to define the developments in architecture and interior design that originated in modernism but began to diverge from that style. Unlike modernism, it includes ornamentation and uses historical references that are often whimsically out of context.

Primary Color: Red, blue, or yellow that can't be produced in pigments by mixing other colors. Primaries plus black and white, in turn, combine to make all the other hues.

Secondary Color: A mix of two primaries. The secondary colors are orange, green, and purple.

Sectional: Furniture made into separate pieces that coordinate with each other. The pieces can be arranged together as a large unit or independently.

Slipcover: A fabric or plastic cover that can be draped or tailored to fit over a piece of furniture.

Stud: A vertical support element made of wood or metal that is used in the construction of walls.

Task Lighting: Lighting that concentrates in specific areas for tasks, such as preparing food, applying makeup, reading, or doing crafts.

Tone: Degree of lightness or darkness of a color.

Tongue-and-Groove Joinery: A joinery technique in which a protruding end (tongue) fits into a recess (groove), locking the two pieces together.

Track Lighting: Lighting that utilizes a fixed band that supplies a current to movable light fixtures.

Trompe L'oeil: Literally meaning "fool the eye"; a painted mural in which realistic images and the illusion of more space are created.

Tufting: The fabric of an upholstered piece or a mattress that is drawn tightly to secure the padding, creating regularly spaced indentations.

Turning: Wood that is cut on a lathe into a round object with a distinctive profile. Furniture legs, posts, rungs, etc., are usually made in this way.

Uplight: Also used to describe the lights themselves, this is actually the term for light that is directed upward toward the ceiling.

Valance: Short drapery that hangs along the top of a window, with or without a curtain underneath.

Value: In relation to a scale of grays ranging from black to white, this is the term to describe the lightness (tints) or darkness (shades) of a color.

Vanity: a bathroom floor cabinet that usually contains a sink and storage space.

Veneer: High-quality wood that is cut into very thin sheets for use as a surface material.

Wainscotting: A wallcovering of boards, plywood, or paneling that covers the lower section of an interior wall and usually contrasts with the wall surface above.

Welt: A cord, often covered by fabric, that is used as an elegant trim on cushions, slipcovers, etc.

Work Triangle: The area bounded by the lines that connect the sink, range, and refrigerator. A kitchen may have multiple work triangles. In an ideal triangle, the distances between appliances are from 4 to 9 feet.

Index

A

Accenting, gold-leaf, 288
Accent lighting, 64, 279
Accessories
  in achieving balance, 16
  art and, 70-77
  in contemporary style, 42
  as storage option, 61
Ambient lighting, 64, 279
Amenities in bedroom,
    244
American country style,
    45, 147
  kitchen in, 144, 148
American traditional
    kitchen, 138
Analogous color scheme,
    20, 21
Arbor designs, 296
Arches in kitchen, 142-43,
    147
Architectural molding, 75
Architectural styles, 289
American traditional, 138
Arts and Crafts-style, 144, 181
  contemporary, 10-11,
      42-43, 154-61, 197
  correcting flaws, 80-81
  cottage style, 146-47, 197
  country, 26, 44-45, 144-
      51, 197, 202-3
American, 45, 144, 147, 148
English, 149
French, 44, 63, 193
  craftsman, 124
  details in, 288
  eclectic, 152-53
  as focal point, 121
Old World, 143, 150-51,

197, 204-5
  retro modern, 155, 156-
      57
  traditional, 138-43, 197
Victorian style, 144, 197,
    206-7
Architectural trim in
    kitchen, 183
Armoires, 48
  corner bar in, 115
  as focal point, 121
  pull-out drawers in, 135
Art
  accessories and, 70-77
  arrangement of, 76-77
  in creating illusion of win
      dows, 130
  lighting for, 65
  selecting, 72
Arts and Crafts-style kitchen,
    144
  cabinets in, 181
Asymmetry, 14
  for hearth, 15

B

Baby rooms, 260-67
  color for, 261
  essentials for, 264-67
  furniture in, 267
Backsplash tiles, 158
Balance, 10, 14, 287
  accessories in achieving, 16
Balloon shades, 89
Bars
  corner, in armoire, 115
  custom-made, 133
Baseboards in kitchens, 183
Basic color scheme, 20

Baskets in bathroom, 203
Bathrooms, 194-235
  baskets in, 203
  blinds in, 234
  cabinets in, 201
  framed, 219
  frameless, 219
  chandeliers in, 67
  color scheme in, 226-27, 231
  contemporary, 197
  country cottage casual,
      197, 202-3
  curtains in, 235
  café, 234
  tie-back, 235
  defining look, 196-207
  faucets in, 198, 201
  fixtures in, 198, 208-15
  furniture in, 203, 218,
      222-25
  lavs in, 210-13
  lighting in, 198, 201, 205
  master, 101
  matching suites in, 224-25
  moisture concerns in, 229
  Old World style, 197, 204-5
  paint/painting, 229
  patterns in, 230-31
  shades in, 234, 235
  pleated, 235
  shutters in, 234, 235
  size of, 194-95, 195
  storage in, 203
  tilework in, 207
  toilets in, 208, 214-15
  traditional, 197
  vanities in, 216-21, 218
  Victorian, 197, 206-7
  wallcoverings in, 228-29,

235
   walls in, 226-27, 226-31
   window treatments in, 232-35
Bay window as focal point, 141
Bead-board ceiling, 290
Bedrooms, 236-67
   accessories in, 240
   amenities in, 244
   baby, 260-67
   bed as focal point in, 239
   buying quality mattress, 58-59, 242
   children's, 250-59
   color for, 237, 239, 240
   computers in, 240
   functionality of, 237, 248
   furniture in, 49, 240
   guest, 248-49
   lighting in, 240, 247
   loft area in, 247
   master, 239, 247
   multitasking and, 237
   as sanctuary, 239-40
   sitting area in, 245
   television in, 240
   walls in, 98
   wall-to-wall carpeting, 239
   window treatments in, 239
Beds
   bunk, 58
   buying mattress for, 58-59, 242
   convertible sofa, 58-59
   day, 58-59
   vintage, 242
Billiards room, 130
Black, painting walls, 130
Blinds, 80, 91

   in bathrooms, 234
   custom, 91
   inside mount for, 82
   outside mount for, 82
   vinyl, 91
   wooden, 82-83, 91
Blue, 28, 30-31
Bookcases, 11, 61
   building basic, 277
   in home office, 273, 277, 280-81
Books
   care of, 280
   shelves for, 11
Brocade, 85
Buffets, 61
Built-in cabinetry, 11
   as focal points, 121
Built-ins, 11, 51, 121
   paint/painting, 61
Bunk beds, 58
Butler's pantry, 162

C

Cabinets, 49, 61
Arts and Crafts-style, 181
   in bathroom, 201
   built-in, 11, 121
   china, 61
   custom, 173
   door style choices for, 166
   framed versus frameless construction, 170-71, 219
   in kitchen, 140-41, 142-43, 147, 148, 149, 161, 162-75
   knock-down, 173
   options for, 168-69
   semi-custom, 135, 173
   shopping for quality, 166-

67, 168
   specialized, 167
Café curtains in bathrooms, 234
Cambric, 85
Candlestick lamp, 71
Canister lighting, 64
Canvas, 85
Carpet runners, 40, 110
Carpets, 110-11
   pile of, 111
   stain protection of, 111
   wall-to-wall, 111, 239
Casegoods, 51
Casings
   door, 186-87
   window, 186-87
Casters, 50
Ceilings
   bead-board, 290
   for kitchens, 190-91
   paint/painting, 96
   raising height of, 15
   tray, 247
   visually raising height of, 15
Cellular shades, 89
Ceramic-tile floor, 108-9, 188-89
Chairs, club, 50
Chaise lounges, 58
Chandeliers
   in bathroom, 67
   in dining room, 65
   in kitchen, 138, 142
Chemical strippers, 289
Children's bedrooms, 250-59
   bedding in, 251
   color in, 254-55
   furniture in, 251-52

Index

storage in, 257
theme in, 251-52, 257-58
China cabinet, 61
Chintz, 85
Cinched shades, 89
Classic-white kitchen, 160-61
Clean-up center in kitchen, 168
Club chairs, 50
Color, 10, 18, 19, 289
  in bathrooms, 226-27, 231
  in bedrooms, 237, 239, 240
  blue, 15
  in children's bedrooms,
    254-55
  choice of, 10
  cool, 23
  dark, 23
  depth of, 38
  in family rooms, 122
  in home office, 275
  intensity of, 38
  light, 23
  in living rooms, 118
  in nurseries, 261
  primary, 21
  secondary, 21
  shade of, 37
  size and, 23
  tertiary, 21
  tone of, 37
  warm, 23
Color schemes
  for bathrooms, 231
  monochromatic, 19, 21, 34-
    35, 71
  natural, 34-35
  naturals, 34-35
  neutrals, 34-35, 41
Color wheel, 18, 20
  analogous, 20, 21

basic, 20
complements, 20, 21
harmonious, 21
monochromatic scheme, 21
split complements, 20, 21
tetrad, 20
triad, 20
working with, 21
Columns
Corinthian, 184-85
Doric, 184-85
Ionic, 184-85
  in kitchens, 183, 184-85
Combing, 101
Complements color scheme,
  20, 21
Computers
  in bedrooms, 240
  in home office, 274
Conservatory, 295
Console, 115
Contemporary homes, 42-43
  baths in, 197
  kitchens in, 154-61
  living rooms in, 10-11
Conversation stations,
  creating, 118
Convertible sofa beds, 58-59
Cooking hearth in kitchen,
  149, 151
Cooktop venting equipment,
  158
Cool colors, 23
Corinthian column, 184-85
Cornices, outside mount for, 82
Cottage style
  bathroom in, 197
  kitchen in, 146-47
Countertops, 138, 139, 149,
  192-93

edge treatments for, 193
engineered stone, 193
granite, 193
marble, 193
natural materials for, 154
slate, 193
soapstone, 193
stainless steel, 193
stone, 193
tiled stone, 19
wood, 193
Country styles, 44-45
  bathrooms in, 197, 202-3
  kitchens in, 144-51
  living room in, 26
Craftsman-style family room,
  124
Creative lighting, 68-69
Cribs, choosing quality, 263
Crown molding in kitchens,
  183
Cupboards, 51
  in kitchen, 140
Curtains
  in bathrooms, 234, 235
  floor-to-ceiling, 19, 25
  length of, 87
  outside mount for, 82
Cushions
  shapes of, 52-53
T-back, 52
Turkish, 52
  tuxedo, 52
Custom cabinets, 173
Custom-made bar, 133
Custom-ordered furniture, 51

D

Damask, 85
Daybeds, 58-59

Deck seating area, 297
Decluttering, 42-43
Decorating
  developing eye for, 9
  patterns in, 25
Decoupage, 100
Depth, 38
Design, 9
  defined, 10
  elements of, 10
Design principles, 14
  balance, 287
  harmony, 287
  line, 287
  proportion, 287
  scale, 287
Desks, 48
Diffused light, 279
Dining rooms
  chairs in, 56, 57
  chandeliers in, 65
Direct light, 279
Door casings
  in kitchen, 186-87
  replacing, 292
Door knockers, 293
Doormat, personalizing, 293
Doors
  antique, 288
  floor-to-ceiling, 128-29
French, 121
  hardware for, 292
  paint/painting, 287
  rectangular panels in, 15
  restoring old, 292
Door trim in kitchen, 183
Doric columns, 184-85
Double-complementary color
  scheme, 21
Double sconces, 69

Dragging, 101
Dressing rooms
  mirrors in, 74-75
  transforming corner into, 239

E
Eclectic kitchen, 152-53
Electronic equipment and
  accessories in living rooms,
  119
Elliptical window, 287
Engineered stone counter
  tops, 193
English country kitchen, 149
Expresso machine, 139, 143

F
Fabrics
  calculating for upholstered
  furniture, 63
  choice of, 10
  for window treatments, 85
Family rooms, 113, 114, 122-
  29
  color of, 122
Craftsman-style, 124
  fireplace in, 124-25, 126-27
  furniture for, 122
  lighting for, 122
  open floor plans for, 128-29
  seating in, 122
  size of, 123, 124
  storage in, 122
  television in, 124, 125
Faucets
  in bathroom, 198, 201
  in kitchen, 148
  satin brass finish for, 201
Faux finish, 96, 178-79
Filing cabinets, 275

Fireplaces, 15, 125, 126-27
  accessories for, 126
  in family room, 124-25, 126-
  27
  as focal points, 121, 124-25
  mantels for, 126
  massive, 11, 15
  materials for, 126
  outdoor, 295
  raised stone, 126
  stacked stone, 126
Fireplace surrounds, marble
  for, 126
Fixtures in bathroom, 198,
  208-15
Flat-screen television, 126
Floor plans, open, 113
  in family rooms, 128-29
  in kitchen, 179
Floors, 79, 104-11
  carpets, 110-11
  ceramic tile, 108-9, 188-89
  in kitchen, 149, 188-89
  linoleum, 188-89
  for porches, 295
  rugs, 110-11
  sheet vinyl, 188-89
  stone, 108
  in sunrooms, 295
  wood, 104-7, 188-89
Floor-to-ceiling curtains, 19, 25
Floor-to-ceiling doors, 128-29
Floral patterns, 25
Foam inserts, 54
Focal points, 77
  armoires as, 121
  bay window as, 141
  bed as, in bedroom, 239
  fireplaces as, 121, 124-25
  in home office, 279

Index

in kitchen, 184-85
in living room, 117, 120-21
Framed cabinets, 170-71
in bathrooms, 219
Frameless cabinets, 170-71
in bathrooms, 219
French-country style, 44, 63, 193
French doors, 121
French traditional style, 141
Front porch
furniture groupings on, 290
wicker on, 290
Front-projection television, 133
Functionality of bedrooms, 237, 248
Furnishings, 46-77
art and accessories as, 70-77
buying quality mattress, 58-59, 242
creating storage, 60-61
furniture, 48-55
lighting, 64-69
reusing old furniture, 62-63
seating, 56-57
Furniture
in bathrooms, 203, 218, 222-25
in bedrooms, 49, 58-59, 240
children's, 251-52
casters for, 50
covering of, 54
custom-ordered, 51
in family rooms, 122
functions of, 49, 115
groupings of, on porch, 290
in home offices, 273
in living rooms, 49, 115-16
making decisions on, 49

in media rooms, 135
metal, 55
modular, 49, 51
moveable, 51
in nurseries, 267
oversized, 116-17
on porches, 284, 290, 291, 294, 295
quality of, 54
ready-to-assemble, 51
reusing old, 63
scale of room in choosing, 13
size of, 49
for sleeping, 58-59
for sunrooms, 294, 295
symmetrical arrangement of, 15
types and terms of, 51
upholstered, 50, 52-53, 55
wood, 54
Furniture-style vanities, 218

G

Gambrel roof, 287
Garden rooms, creating entry into, 296
Gathering places, 113
General light, 64, 279
Gingham, 85
Glazed tiles, 108
Gold-leaf accenting, 288
Granite countertops, 193
Great rooms, 122, 128-29
Green, 32-33, 39
Groupings, furniture, 290
Guest rooms, 248-49

H

Hallway, walls in, 98
Hardscaping, 287

Hardware
for doors, 292
in kitchen, 141
for windows, 87, 94-95
Harmonious color scheme, 21
Harmony, 10, 14, 287
Hearth, asymmetrical, 15
Heat gun, 289
Home offices, 168, 268, 270-81
bookcases in, 273, 277, 280-81
color in, 275
computers in, 274
decorating, 273
focal point in, 279
furniture in, 273
lighting in, 278-79
seating in, 270
sliding wall panels in, 274
storage in, 273, 274-75
wall treatment in, 273
workspace in, 270-71, 274
Horizontal lines, 287
Horizontal stripes, 11
House numbers, 293
Hutches, 48

I

Indirect light, 279
Intensity, 38
Ionic columns, 184-85
Islands in kitchen, 140, 147, 148

J

Jabot, 80, 82-83

K

Kitchens, 136-93

American farmhouse, 148
  arches in, 142, 143, 147
Arts and Crafts style, 144
  backsplash tiles in, 158
  baseboards in, 183
  bay window as focal point in, 141
  cabinets in, 140-41, 142-43, 147, 148, 149, 161, 162-75
  ceilings for, 190-91
  chandeliers in, 138, 142
  classic-white, 160-61
  clean-up center in, 168
  columns in, 183, 184-85
  contemporary, 154-61
  cooking hearth in, 149
  cooktop venting equipment in, 158
  cottage style, 146-47
  countertops in, 138, 139, 149, 154, 192-93
  country, 144-51
  crown molding in, 183
  cupboards in, 140
  door casings in, 186-87
  door trim in, 183
  eclectic, 152-53
English country, 149
  faucets in, 148
  floors in, 149, 188-89
  focal point in, 141, 184-85
French traditional, 141
  hardware in, 141
  islands in, 140, 147, 148
  lighting in, 67, 69
  offices in, 268, 282-83
Old World style, 150-51
  open-plan, 179
  range hood in, 174-75
Retro Modern, 156-57

style of, 136
tiled countertops in, 19
traditional, 138-43
trimwork in, 182-83
wall treatments in, 177-87
window casings in, 186-87
windows in, 161, 183
Knock-down cabinets, 173

L
Lace, 85
Laminates, wood, 104
Lamps, candlestick, 71
Lampshades, selecting right, 66-67
Landscaping, 287
Layout, 49
Library, wallpaper in, 98
Lighting, 64-69
  accent, 64, 279
  ambient, 64, 279
  for art, 65
  in bathrooms, 198, 201, 205
  in bedrooms, 240, 247
  canister, 64
  chandeliers as, 65, 67, 138, 142
  creative, 68-69
  cylindrical, 287
  diffused, 279
  direct, 279
  in family rooms, 122
  formulating successful plan, 64
  general, 64
  in home offices, 278-79
  indirect, 279
  in kitchens, 67, 69
  in media rooms, 132, 133
  natural, 64, 96

overhead, 11
pendant, 69
for porches, 294
portrait, 69
selecting right lampshade, 66-67
for sunrooms, 294, 295
task, 279
under-cabinetry, 69
Linens, 85
  choosing, 242
Lines, 10, 14, 287
  in decorating, 118
  horizontal, 287
  play of, 43
  vertical, 287
Linoleum, 188-89
Living rooms, 113, 114-21
  anchoring arrangement, 118
  beauty tips for, 118
  color in, 118
  contemporary, 10-11
  conversation stations in, 118
  country, 26
  curing clutter, 118
  electronic equipment and accessories in, 119
  focal point for, 117, 120-21
  formal air of, 41
  furniture for, 49, 115-16
  providing continuity with color, 118
  reading between lines, 118
  seating area in, 119
  sightlines in, 120-21
  style of, 114
Loft area in bedroom, 247
Loveseat, 56, 57, 115
L-shaped seating arrange ment, 57

Index

M

Marble
  for countertops, 193
  for fireplace, 126
  for floors, 108
Master bathrooms, 101
Master bedrooms, 239, 247
Materials, diversity in, 42
Mattress
  buying quality, 58-59
  choosing, 242
Media rooms, 113, 132-35
  area for, 132, 133
  equipment for, 132, 133
  furniture for, 134-35
  lighting in, 132, 133
  storage in, 135
  temperature control for, 132
Metal furniture, 55
Mid-century modern style,
  influence on kitchen design,
  155
Mirrored screen, 117
Mirrors, 74-75
  antique, 74
Modular furniture, 49, 51
Moiré, 85
Moisture in bathrooms, 229
Monochromatic color scheme,
  19. 71, 21, 34-35
Moveable furniture, 51
Multifunctional spaces, 113
Multitasking of bedrooms, 237
Muntins on the patio doors,
  139
Murals for walls, 102-3
Muslin, 85

N

Natural color schemes, 34-35
Natural light, 64, 96
Neutral color scheme, 34-35,
  41
Notebook, compiling a design,
  12
Nurseries, 260-67
  color for, 261
  essentials for, 264-67
  furniture in, 267

O

Old World style
  in bathroom, 197, 204-5
  in kitchen, 143, 150-51
Open floor plans, 113
  in family rooms, 128-29
  in kitchen, 179
Orange, 29
Organdy, 85
Ottomans, 115, 135
  tufted, 63
Outdoors, 284-97
  arbors in, 296
  fireplaces in, 295
  furniture on porch, 284
  ornamentation in, 287
  slipcovers for seating pieces
  in, 291
  trellises in, 296, 297
Overhead lighting, 11
Oversized furniture, 116-17

P

Painted effects for walls, 100-
  101
Painted floorcloth, 110
Paint/painting

in bathrooms, 229
of built-ins, 61
of ceilings, 96
of doors, 287
in porch, 287
stripping layers of, 289
as wall treatment, 96
of wicker, 297
Paneling in kitchens, 177
Pantry, butler's, 162
Parquet flooring, 107
Pastels, 36-37
Patio doors, muntins on, 139
Patterns, 10, 18, 19
  in bathrooms, 230-31
  in decorating, 25
  floral, 25
  small-scale, 25
Pedestal sinks, 210
Pelmet, 92
Pendant lights, 69
Pendants, 67
Pergola roof, 297
Personal touches, 40
Piano, 117
Picture window as focal points,
  121
Pilaster construction, 184-85
Pillows
  choosing, 242
  throw, 244
Plan(s)
  developing written, 12
  open floor, 113, 128-29, 179
Plantation shutters, 91
Porches, 294-97
  adding warmth to, 288
  front, 290
  furniture on, 284, 290, 291,

lighting for, 294
purposes of, 291
style of, 291
wraparound, 290
Portrait lights, 69
Primary colors, 21
Privacy hedge, planting, 294
Proportion, 10, 11, 14, 16, 287
Purple, 30-31
Putty knife, 289

Q
Quality
choosing, for crib, 263
of furniture, 54
of mattress, 58-59, 242

R
Ragging off, 101
Ragging on, 101
Raised stone fireplaces, 126
Range hood, 174-75
Ready-to-assemble furniture,
51
Recreation room, 130-31
Red, 28, 29
Retro modern kitchen, 155,
156-57
Rhythm, 10, 14
Roller shades, 89
Roman shades, 80, 89, 133
Roofs
gambrel, 287
pergola, 297
Room-darkening shades, 89
Rugs, 110-11
Rusticated stone wall, 178

S
Satin, 85

Scale, 10, 11, 14, 16, 287
in choosing furniture, 13
Scalloped valances, 92
Sconces, 67
double, 69
Scraper blade, 289
Seating, 51, 57
in family rooms, 122
in home office, 270
in living rooms, 119
Secondary colors, 21
Sectional, dividing, 57
Semicustom cabinets, 135,
173
Shades, 37, 89, 291
balloon, 89
in bathrooms, 234, 235
cellular, 89
cinched, 89
finishing, 89
inside mount for, 82
outside mount for, 82
roller, 89
Roman, 80, 89, 133
room-darkening, 89
special, 91
Shaver, Rick, 152
Sheet vinyl flooring, 188-89
Shoji screens, 91
Shutters, 80, 91
in bathrooms, 234, 235
plantation, 91
Sightlines, 121
Silk, 85
Simplicity, 42-43
Sinks
in bathrooms, 210-13
pedestal, 210
Sitting area in bedroom, 245
Size

color and, 23
of family rooms, 123, 124
Skylight, 73
Slate
for countertops, 193
for floors, 108
Sleeping, furniture for, 58-59
Slipcovers for outdoor seating
pieces, 291
Small-scale patterns, 25
Soapstone countertops, 193
Sofa beds, convertible, 58-59
Sofas, 115
oversize, 49
upholstered, 53
Space
accessing your, 12-13
breaking up, 16
dividing up, 13
Split complements color
scheme, 20
Sponging, 101
Stacked stone fireplaces, 126
Stained-glass window, 288
Stainless steel countertops,
193
Staircase, winding iron, 247
Stenciling, 101
Stippling, 101
Stone
for countertops, 193
for floors, 108
Storage, 61
in bathrooms, 203
in children's bedrooms, 257
in family rooms, 122
in home offices, 274-75
in media rooms, 135
Style, 40-45
of porch, 291

Index

of porch, 291
Sunporch, 117
Sunrooms, 294-97
  furniture for, 294, 295
  lighting for, 294
  windows and skylights in, 295
Swags, 80, 82-83
Symmetry, 14, 287
  in arranging furniture, 15, 16

T

Tactile interest, 26
Taffeta, 85
Tapestry, 77
Task lighting, 279
T-back cushion, 52
Television
  in bedrooms, 240
  in family rooms, 124, 125
  flat-screen, 126
  front-projection, 133
  niche for, 125
Tension rods, inside mount for, 82
Tertiary colors, 21
Tetrad color scheme, 20
Textiles, 77
Texture, 10, 18, 19, 26
Theme in children's bedrooms, 251-52, 257-58
Throw pillows, 244
Tiles
  glazed, 108
  unglazed, 108
Toile de Jouy, 85
Toilets in bathrooms, 208, 214-15
Tone, 37

Tone-on-tone, 34
Traditional baths, 197
Traditional kitchens, 138-43
Traffic patterns, 57
Tray ceiling, 247
Trellis, 297
  designs of, 296
Triad color scheme, 20
Trimwork, profiles in, 182-83
Trompe l'oeil, 101, 102-3
Turkish cushion, 52
Tuxedo cushion, 52

U

Under-cabinetry lighting, 69
Unglazed tiles, 108
Upholstered furniture, 52-53, 55
  calculating yardage for, 63
Upholstered sofas, 53
U-shaped seating
  arrangement, 57

V

Valances, 80
  distinctive, 92-93
  scalloped, 92
Vanities
  in bathrooms, 216-21
  built-in, 61
  framed versus frameless, 219
  furniture-style, 218
Velvet, 85
Vertical lines, 287
Victorian style
  bathroom in, 197, 206-7
  kitchen in, 144
  Vinyl blinds, 91

W

Wallcoverings, 98-99, 177, 181
  in bathrooms, 228-29, 235
  period, 98
  textured vinyl, 99
  tone-on-tone, 99
Wall panels, sliding, in home offices, 274
Wall-to-wall carpet, 111, 239
Wall treatments, 96-103
  in bathrooms, 226-31
  faux finish, 179
  in kitchens, 177-87
  murals for, 102-3
  painted effects for, 100-101
  painting, 96, 130, 177, 181
  paneling, 177
  rusticated stone, 178
  wallcoverings, 98-99, 177, 181
Warm colors, 23
Wicker
  on front porch, 290
  paint/painting, 294
Winding iron staircase, 247
Window bench, 261
Window casings in kitchen, 186-87
Windows, 78-95
  bay, 141
  elliptical, 287
  equalizing, 86-87
  in kitchen, 161
  measuring, 82-83
  oval shaped, 287
  picture, 121
  stained-glass, 288
  in sunrooms, 295

in bathroom, 232-35
in bedrooms, 239
blinds as, 80, 82-83, 91, 234
curtains as, 19, 25, 87, 234, 235
fabric for, 85
hardware for, 87, 94-95
jabots as, 80, 82-83
shades as, 37, 80, 89, 91, 133, 234, 235, 291
shutters as, 80, 91, 234, 235
swags as, 80, 82-83
valances as, 80, 92-93

Window trim in kitchen, 183
Wood countertops, 193
Wooden blinds, 82-83, 91
Wood floors, 104-7, 188-89
  color, grain, and imperfections, 107
  creativity for, 106
  stains for, 107
  types of wood, 107
Wood furniture, 54
Wood laminates, 104
Workspaces, 268-83
  in home office, 270-71, 274

in kitchen office, 282-83
Wraparound porch, 290

Y

Yardage, calculating, for upholstered furniture, 63
Yellow, 32-33

Photo Credits

All photography by Mark Samu, unless otherwise noted.

page 1: courtesy of Thibaut, collection: Equestrian/Castle Pine **pages 3–4:** design: Eileen Boyd Interiors **pages 6:** top left builder: Witt Construction **pages 8–9:** courtesy of Hearst Magazines **page 14:** design: Steven Goldgram Design **pages 16–18:** all design: Eileen Boyd Interiors **page 19:** top design: Eileen Boyd Interiors **page 21:** right design: Lucianna Samu Design/Benjamin Moore Paint **page 22:** courtesy of Hearst Magazines **pages 24–25:** top right courtesy of Thibaut, collection: Picking Flowers/Sweet Life; all others design: Eileen Boyd Interiors **page 26:** left courtesy of Thibaut, collection: Alligator/Texture Resource; right courtesy of Thibaut, collection: Grass Weave/Texture Resource **page 27:** courtesy of Thibaut, collection Ashville/Castle Pine **page 28:** top right courtesy of Thibaut, collection: Sheffield/Sweet Life; bottom right design: Lucianna Samu Design/Benjamin Moore Paint **page 30:** top left builder: Hummel Construction, architect: Donald Billinkoff AIA; bottom design: Eileen Boyd Interiors **page 31:** courtesy of Thibaut, collection: Nantucket/Sweet Life **page 32:** top left design: Lee Najman Design; bottom design: Sherrill Canet Design **pages 34–35:** top right design: Artistic Designs by Deidre; bottom right courtesy of Thibaut, collection: South Beach/Sweet Life; bottom middle & bottom left courtesy of Hearst Magazines; top left courtesy of Thibaut, collection: Sagri/Texture Resource; top middle builder: Bonacio Construction **page 36:** courtesy of Thibaut, collection: Molinia/Texture Resource **page 37:** top courtesy of Thibaut, collection: Window Shop/Sweet Life; bottom right courtesy of Hearst Magazines; bottom left architect: Robert Storm Architects **page 38:** top both courtesy of Hearst Magazines **page 39:** design: Steven Goldgram Design **pages 42–43:** all builder: Hummel Construction, architect: Donald Billinkoff AIA **page 44:** left design: Lucianna Samu Design/Benjamin Moore Paint; right courtesy of Thibaut, collection: Pheasant Toile/Castle Pine **page 45:** top courtesy of Hearst Magazines; bottom right design: Riverside Furniture **page 48:** courtesy of Ballard Designs **page 49:** left courtesy of Ethan Allen; right courtesy of Thibaut, collection: St. James/Castle Pine **page 50:** top architect: Bruce Nagle AIA; bottom builder: Hummel Construction, architect: Donald Billinkoff AIA

page 51: left courtesy of Thibaut, collection: Telluride/Castle Pine; right courtesy of Ethan Allen **page 52:** courtesy of Hearst Magazines **page 53:** top courtesy of Hearst Magazines **page 54:** design: Riverside Furniture **page 55:** top right design: Carolyn Miller Design; bottom design: Hudson Interiors **page 56:** courtesy of Thibaut, collection: Picking Flowers/Sweet Life **page 57:** courtesy of Thibaut, collection: South Beach/Sweet Life **page 59:** courtesy of Thibaut, collection: Javonica/Texture Resource **page 60:** design: Lee Najman Design **page 61:** bottom design: C. Gottlieb **pages 62–63:** all design: Linda Correia Design **page 64:** design: Linda Correia Design **page 65:** right design: Patrick Falco Design; bottom left design: Linda Correia Design; top left design: Thomas Lighting **page 66:** top design: Eileen Boyd Interiors; bottom both courtesy of Hearst Magazines **page 67:** top courtesy of Schonbek Worldwide Lighting; bottom left courtesy of Artemide **page 68:** design Lucianna Samu Design **page 69:** courtesy of Seagull Lighting **page 70:** courtesy of Thibaut, collection: Appalachia/Texture Resource **page 71:** top Donald Billinkoff AIA; bottom courtesy of Ballard Designs **page 72:** design: Donald Billinkoff AIA **page 74:** top builder: Durst Construction; bottom right design: Sherrill Canet Design **page 75:** right design: Eileen Boyd Interiors **page 76:** top right courtesy of Thibaut, collection: Venetian/Texture Resource; bottom right design: Steven Goldgram Design; bottom left builder: Durst Construction; top left design: Pascucci Deslisle Design **page 78:** design: Courland Design **page 80:** left design: Ken Kelly; right cabinet: Kraftmaid Cabinetry **page 81:** design: Sherrill Canet Design **page 83:** left design-build: Benvenuti & Stein; top right design: Jeanne Leonard **page 84:** design: Perfect Interiors **page 87:** left design: Sherrill Canet Design; right courtesy of Hunter Douglas **page 88:** top right design: Correia Design; bottom right & bottom left courtesy of Hunter Douglas; top left builder: D. Reis Construction **page 89:** design: Saratoga Signature Interiors **page 90:** top right builder: T. Michaels Contracting; all others courtesy of Hunter Douglas **page 91:** courtesy of Hunter Douglas **page 93:** design: Tom Edwards **page 94:** left design: Eileen Boyd Interiors; right courtesy of Hearst Magazines **page 95:** top right design: Eileen Boyd Interiors; bottom design: Sherrill Canet Design; top left courtesy of Hearst Magazines **page 96:** top

architect: Bruce Nagle AIA **page 97:** both design: Mary Melissa **pages 98–99:** top right design: Healing Bursanti; bottom right & bottom left design: Sherrill Canet Design; top left & top middle design: Lucianna Samu Design **page 100:** top both design: Schuyler Pond **page 101:** both design: Deidre Gatta Design **page 102:** design: Ellen Roche **page 103:** all design: Susan Wiley **pages 104–105:** design: Lucianna Samu Design/Benjamin Moore Paint **page 106:** top left design: Artistic Designs by Deidre; top right design: Lucianna Samu Design **page 108:** builder: Hummel Construction, architect: Donald Billinkoff AIA **page 109:** top design: Kitchens by Ken Kelly; bottom right design: Kitchen Dimensions **page 110:** top right design: Patrick Falco Design; bottom right builder: Hummel Construction, architect: Donald Billinkoff AIA; top left design: Schuyler Pond **page 111:** bottom builder: D. Reis Construction **pages 114–115:** all design: Linda Correia Design **pages 116–117:** all design: Linda Correia Design **pages 118–119:** all design-build: Benvenuti & Stein **page 120:** both design: Carpen House **page 121:** both builder: Durst Construction **page 122:** both builder: T. Michaels Contracting **page 123:** architect: Brian Shore AIA **pages 124–125:** top right & bottom right builder: Durst Construction; middle architect: Andy Levtovsky; bottom left & top left builder: Bonacio Construction **page 126:** top architect: Andy Levtovsky; bottom design: Courland Design **page 127:** architect: Andy Levtovsky **pages 128–129:** all builder: Bonacio Construction **pages 130–131:** left builder: Bonacio Construction; middle builder: Hummel Construction, architect: Donald Billinkoff AIA; bottom right builder: Witt Construction **pages 132–133:** all design: TJK Interiors **pages 134:** top courtesy of LA-Z-Boy **page 135:** courtesy of KraftMaid Cabinetry **pages 138–139:** center, top right, bottom center & bottom left design: Ken Kelly; bottom right Builder Architect Magazine **pages 140–141:** all builder: T. Michaels Contracting **pages 142–145:** all design: Jean Stoffer **pages 146–147:** center, bottom center, bottom left & top left design: Kitchen Dimensions **page 148:** design: KraftMaid **page 149:** top design: Eileen Boyd; bottom courtesy of Crossville **pages 150–151:** all design: Jean Stoffer **pages 152–153:** all design: Patrick Falco **pages 154–155:** all styling: Tia Burns **pages 156–157:** all design: Ken Kelly **pages 158–159:** center design: Andy Levtovsky, A.I.A.; top right &

bottom right design: Bruce Nagle, A.I.A.; bottom left builder: Bonacio Construction **page 160:** design: Jim DeLuca, A.I.A. **page 162:** design: Kitty McCoy, A.I.A. **page 163:** builder: Access Builders **page 164:** top & bottom right design: Ken Kelly; bottom left design: Jean Stoffer **page 165:** top right design: The Breakfast Room; left center design: Jean Stoffer **page 166:** left center & right center design: Kitty McCoy, A.I.A.; bottom courtesy of KraftMaid **page 167:** left design: Ken Kelly; right design: Kitty McCoy, A.I.A. **pages 168–169:** top center builder: Gold Coast Construction; top right courtesy of Hearst Magazines; bottom right design: Montlor Box, A.I.A.; bottom center builder: Gold Coast Construction; bottom left, left center & top left design: Ken Kelly **page 170:** top courtesy of Hearst Magazines; bottom right design: Ken Kelly; bottom left builder: T. Michaels Contracting **page 171:** courtesy of Plain & Fancy **page 172:** courtesy of KraftMaid **page 173:** top right design: Mojo-Stumer, A.I.A.; bottom right architect: SD Atelier, A.I.A.; top left design: Habitech **page 174:** top left courtesy of Wolf; bottom left design: Delisle/Pascucci **page 175:** top left & top right design: Ken Stoffer; bottom right design: The Breakfast Room; bottom left builder: Access Builders **page 176:** design: Ken Kelly **page 178:** top right & bottom right courtesy of Hearst Magazines; left photo: Don Wong/CH, painting: Dee Painting & Faux Finishes **page 179:** top right design: Montlor Box, A.I.A.; bottom right design: Linda Correia Designs Ltd. **page 180:** top right design: Patrick Falco; bottom courtesy of Glidden; top left design: Sherrill Canet **page 181:** courtesy of Sherwin Williams **pages 182–183:** bottom right builder: Bonacio Construction; top center & top left design: Ken Kelly **page 184:** top right builder: T. Michaels Contracting; bottom design: Paula Yedyank; top left design: Jean Stoffer **page 185:** design: Eileen Boyd Interiors **page 187:** top design: Andy Levtovsky, A.I.A.; bottom right & bottom left courtesy of Thibaut **page 188:** courtesy of Armstrong **page 189:** top left architect: SD Atelier, A.I.A.; bottom courtesy of Armstrong **page 190:** design: Kitty McCoy, A.I.A. **page 191:** top courtesy of Above View; bottom right & bottom left courtesy of Armstrong **pages 192–193:** top center courtesy of Formica; right, bottom right & bottom left courtesy of Corian; top left design: Ken Kelly **page 194:** design: Sherrill Canet Design **page 196:** top design: KraftMaid; bottom courtesy of Hearst Magazines **page**

197: top design: Deidre Gatta; bottom right design: The Tile Studio; bottom left design: Lee Najman **page 198:** top left courtesy of Ginger; top right courtesy of Sonoma; bottom left courtesy of MGS **page 199:** design: Lee Najman **pages 200–201:** left courtesy of Hearst Magazines; top courtesy of Bach; bottom right builder: T. Michaels Contracting; bottom center courtesy of Seagull Lighting **page 202:** design: KraftMaid **page 203:** top left design: Mojo-Stumer, A.I.A.; bottom left courtesy of Hearst Magazines **pages 204–205:** all design: The Tile Studio **pages 206–207:** all design: Deidre Gatta **page 208:** top design: Ken Kelly; bottom builder: Dean Durst Construction **page 209:** top right courtesy of Sonoma; bottom builder: Bonacio Construction **pages 210–211:** top left courtesy of Sonoma; top left center design: Deidre Gatta; left design: The Tile Studio; bottom center courtesy of Hearst Magazines; bottom left courtesy of Sonoma **page 212:** top left design: Sherrill Canet; bottom left courtesy of Kohler **page 213:** top design: Lucianna Samu Design; bottom courtesy of Adagio **page 214:** top left courtesy of Kohler; top right courtesy of Neo-Metro; bottom courtesy of Herbeau **page 215:** top left courtesy of Neo-Metro; right courtesy of Herbeau; bottom courtesy of Neo-Metro **page 216:** courtesy of Merillat **page 217:** top courtesy of Wood-Mode; bottom right design: Jeanne Leonard **page 218:** right design: The Tile Studio; right design: Sherrill Canet **page 219:** top left & top right courtesy of Wood-Mode; bottom right & bottom left courtesy of KraftMaid **page 220:** builder: T. Michaels Contracting **page 221:** top left & top right design: The Tile Studio; bottom design: Anne Tarasoff **pages 222–223:** top left design: Jeanne Leonard; bottom center design: Lucianna Samu Design; left design: Deidre Gatta **page 224:** top & bottom courtesy of Merillat **page 225:** top courtesy of Merillat; bottom courtesy of KraftMaid **pages 226–227:** top center design: Sherrill Canet; top right courtesy of Glidden; bottom right design: Lucianna Samu Design; bottom center courtesy of Sherwin Williams; left courtesy of Hearst Magazines **pages 228–229:** top center builder: Dean Durst Construction; bottom right courtesy of Schonbek Worldwide Lighting, Inc. **pages 230–231:** top left & inset builder: T. Michaels Contracting; right courtesy of York Wallcoverings **page 232:** George Ross/CH **page 233:** top left design: Mojo-Stumer, A.I.A.; top right & bottom right courtesy of Hearst

Magazines **page 234:** left design: SD Atelier, A.I.A.; top right courtesy of Motif Designs; bottom courtesy of Hearst Magazines **page 235:** top left design: Ken Kelly; bottom right design: Doug Moyer, A.I.A. **pages 236–237:** design: Rinaldi Associates **pages 238–239:** all design: Anne Tarasoff **page 240:** left courtesy of Thibaut, collection: Scottish Plaid/Castle Pine; right design: Patrick Falco **page 241:** design: Patrick Falco **page 243:** design: Lee Najman Design **page 244:** top design: Denise Maurer; bottom courtesy of Hearst Magazines **page 245:** all courtesy of Hearst Magazines **page 246:** design: Lee Najman Design **page 247:** top right courtesy of Hearst Magazines, painting: Inpaint Workshops & Studio, furniture: Choice Seating; bottom design: Pascucci Deslisle Design; top left courtesy of Hearst Magazines **pages 248–249:** all builder: Hummel Construction, architect: Donald Billinkoff AIA **pages 260–261:** design: Pascucci Deslisle Design **page 262:** courtesy of Thibaut, collection: Carnival/Toile Resource **page 263:** left courtesy of York Wallcoverings; right courtesy of Seabrook Wallcoverings **page 264:** top courtesy of York Wallcoverings; bottom design: Picture Perfect Design **page 265:** courtesy of York Wallcoverings **page 266:** courtesy of Finn + Hattie **page 267:** courtesy of Seabrook Wallcoverings **pages 268–269:** builder: Gold Coast Construction **pages 270–271:** both design: Lee Najman Design **page 273:** design: Ken Kelly **page 274:** top right courtesy of Ballard Designs; bottom right courtesy of Ethan Allen; top left courtesy of Hearst Magazines **page 275:** both courtesy of Elfa/The Container Store **page 278:** bottom left design: Patrick Falco **page 280:** builder: Witt Construction **page 281:** design: Lucianna Samu Design **page 283:** top courtesy of Hearst Magazines **pages 286–289:** all Stan Sudol/CH **page 290:** top courtesy of Armstrong Urban Challenge; bottom Stan Sudol/CH **page 291:** Stan Sudol/CH **page 292:** top both courtesy of Atlas **page 293:** top courtesy of Restoration Hardware; bottom Stan Sudol/CH **page 294:** courtesy of Colebrook Conservatories **page 295:** bottom courtesy of Armstrong Urban Challenge; top left design-build: Access Builders **page 296:** top courtesy of Elyria Fence, Inc.; bottom right courtesy of www.gidesigns.net; bottom left courtesy of Trellis Structures **page 297:** top right & bottom right courtesy of Garden Artisans; top left courtesy of Elyria Fence, Inc.

If you like
Design Ideas for Home Decorating,
take a look at the rest of the
Design Idea series

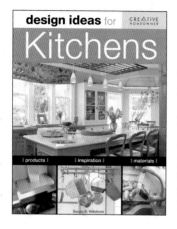

Design Ideas for Kitchens provides design inspiration for creating an attractive, up-to-date kitchen. Contains hundreds of photographs and a wealth of information. *Paper with flaps.*

Over 500 photographs.
224 pp.
$ 19.95 (US)
$ 24.95 (CAN)
BOOK #: 279415

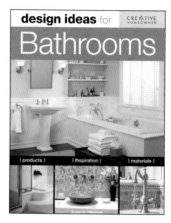

Design Ideas for Bathrooms offers hundreds of color photographs and extensive information on the latest trends in design, materials, and related products. *Paper with flaps.*

Over 500 photographs.
224 pp.
$ 19.95 (US)
$ 24.95 (CAN)
BOOK #: 279268

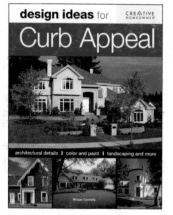

Design Ideas for Curb Appeal shows how to make the outside of the home look its very best. Entryways, windows, siding, landscaping, and more are covered. *Paper with flaps.*

Over 300 photographs.
208 pp.
$ 19.95 (US)
$ 24.95 (CAN)
BOOK #: 274812

Design Ideas for Home Storage is loaded with color photographs and lots of consumer-friendly information on providing both everyday and long-term storage for everything. *Paper with flaps.*

Over 350 photographs.
208 pp.
$ 19.95 (US)
$ 24.95 (CAN)
BOOK #: 279491

Design Ideas for Flooring is the ultimate guide to the latest materials, products, and styles in flooring. Over 350 color photographs. *Paper with flaps.*

Over 450 photographs.
208 pp.
$ 19.95 (US)
$ 24.95 (CAN)
BOOK #: 279242

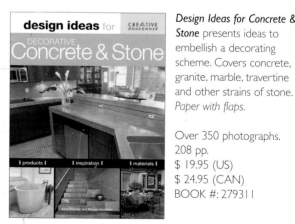

Design Ideas for Concrete & Stone presents ideas to embellish a decorating scheme. Covers concrete, granite, marble, travertine and other strains of stone. *Paper with flaps.*

Over 350 photographs.
208 pp.
$ 19.95 (US)
$ 24.95 (CAN)
BOOK #: 279311

Look for these and other fine **Creative Homeowner books** wherever books are sold.
For more information and to order direct, visit our Web site at
www.creativehomeowner.com